About 1

Donna Kennedy (BA Psych hons, MHGC, MNLP) was born in Co. Mayo, Ireland. She is a bestselling author, qualified psychologist and a highly sought after professional speaker. She started her first business at aged 23 and has gone on to develop several successful businesses since. She has given seminars to thousands of people and companies worldwide and regularly features in national and international media as an expert. She is solution focused and results driven and her reputation for getting clients results has led to her being recognised and cited in international journals and records by leading organisations and faculties.

Donna does not believe in waiting around in the hope of a better life or analysing forever and a day, she embraces every situation with a solution focused approach for best performance. This is evident in her talks, programs and books.

More about Donna

Donna wasn't always the confident woman she is today. At one point in her life her confidence was so low that she was afraid to walk across the street on her own. She endured a huge amount of challenge and suffering during her early years and as such she knows what it is to feel pain. But importantly she knows how to get out of it. Donna walks the talk. She has been there, done that and she has come out the other end successful. Her passion is to teach others to do the same. It is her firm belief that it is not what happens to you in your life that matters as much as what you do with what happens to you.

Acknowledgements

I want to thank: my mother and father, Maureen and Padraic Kennedy, for never giving up on me and encouraging me to be who I am today; my soul mate, Pat Slattery, who lights up my life in so many ways; my son Ashton and his brothers Christopher, Keith and Jason; my brothers and sisters for their understanding and encouragement; my aunts, uncles and cousins for their kindness throughout my recovery; Dr Deirdre Collins and Dr Terence Larkin for their support and kindness; Mary Munroe, Ciara Heneghan, Nicola Coughlan, Michelle Ruane, Karen Brandt, Triona O'Malley, Bernadine Walsh, Susanne Ferris, Paula Gibbons and Elizabeth Ryder for their caring and kindness; Bob Proctor, Teacher in The Secret and best-selling author; Mark Victor-Hansen, Richard Branson, Owen Fitzpatrick, Brian Colbert, John Boyle, Louise Hay and Bill Cullen, for their dedication to inspiring others to live life to the fullest; Liam Lyons for his belief in me when I didn't believe in myself and Patrick Durcan for his support and strength, Joe Griffin and Ivan Tyrell for their dedication to education; Brendan Sands and Eileen Forrestal at Get Up and Go Publications for their professionalism and dedication, Nuala Redmond for cover design, and all my clients for taking action to empower their lives and the lives of those around them.

THE CONFIDENCE TO SUCCEED

The Power to be, do and have all that you deserve in life and business!

Donna Kennedy

Dedicated to my mother,
Maureen Kennedy.

Contents

Introduction

Most people strive to be confident and to attain success of some kind. The world we live in revolves around it. The career we have, the people we know, how much money we have, how we look, how well we perform in sports, how easy we find it to socialize – we are a society of comparisons and benchmarking. We look at other people and dream of having what they have or of being like them, understandably feeling inferior and inadequate in the process. We rarely feel "enough". Well let me tell you a little secret – you are enough and by the time you have finished reading this book, you will know that.

When I was younger, people perceived me to be a successful person who was full of confidence. On the outside I had it all. I was confident, intelligent and successful. I was model-like in appearance and talented in so many ways. The reality however was very different. In fact, it was so different that at one point in my life my confidence was so low that I would have preferred to chew on glass than walk across the street on my own. I hated myself and I hated my life. Whilst other people saw me to be successful, the truth was inside I was dying and I would have preferred to disappear. Having experienced several difficult challenges in my life, I know what it is to feel worthless. I was in fact once afraid of everything and everyone.

Fast-forward to now however, and I have learned what it is to be genuinely confident. And what true success is. I now love life and live it. I am healthy, mind and body. Whereas once I was petrified to speak to anyone or do anything, now I am confident to walk into a crowded room and strike up conversation with whomever I choose. I have no issue whatsoever with confidence, talking to people or being afraid of doing something new or getting hurt. Not only that, my life, both personal and professional, now revolves around interaction with people and change. Every day I am required to meet new people and embrace new situations. I am regularly required to speak on stage in front of thousands of people at a time and to appear on TV and radio, knowing millions of people are watching and listening to me, yet it doesn't bother me in the slightest. In fact I enjoy it! Whereas once I questioned my ability to do everything, now I allow myself to try new things. I can now say with absolute confidence that I'm not afraid to be myself, and that is something I never even dreamed of being able to say or do. In this book I am going to show you exactly *how* I did it, how I bridged the gap between having no confidence and feeling worthless to feeling confident and happy almost every day.

I assume you picked up this book because you or someone you know would like to feel more confident. Maybe you would like to overcome a fear, may be you would like to like yourself more, to feel better about yourself and to know that you are adequate, or maybe you would like to feel more confident around people, perhaps in making friends, developing a relationship or speaking in front of groups. Whatever your reason for picking up this book, you can be guaranteed that I can relate to how you feel. I won't pretend to know exactly how you feel (nobody can) but I certainly know what it is to live the feeling of fear, the feeling of worrying about what to say or do in any given situation, worrying that you have to act or be a certain way to be accepted, the feeling when you cannot stop your body and/or voice from shaking inside (and sometimes outside)... 'Am I good enough?' 'What if they don't like me?' 'What if I mess up?' 'What if I don't perform well?' 'What if I run out of things to say?' 'What if they think I'm stupid?' 'What if they make fun of me?' 'What if I can't handle this or fail?' etc. Not feeling confident is a very difficult thing to endure and as you know, it can have such a devastating impact on your life, but the fact is, I get it! I've lived it. I've suffered it. I've cried it. However, knowing what I know now, my aim in this book is to help you overcome whatever it is you are afraid of or need to feel more confident doing.

The Confidence to Succeed isn't just a confidence book; it is a purposely designed how-to system that has the potential to transform your life, no matter what your current situation or how bad it seems or how long you have endured it. The one thing that used to frustrate me when I read books about confidence and success (I read lots over the years!), is that I was often enlightened but never shown the *how*. I learned lots of fancy information but at the end of each book I was none the wiser as to what specifically I had to do to become confident. *The Confidence to Succeed* goes well beyond theory or ideology; it is a straight forward, give-it-to-me-straight system to get *real life* results *now*. There are exercises along the way that I would like you to complete so you begin to get results straight away. Some of the exercises you will love and some may make you feel temporarily uncomfortable (that's not a bad thing!) but if you use the information in this book as I instruct you to, I promise that you will get excellent results and you will begin to notice a positive difference quite quickly.

But before I show you how to do this, I have just one simple request from you, and that is that you are totally honest with yourself throughout the book. Self-honesty, although not always easy, is the only way to a genuinely confident future. Let's be real here so we get you real results that matter. There is no judgment here, everything in this book is to help you overcome any obstacles you may be experiencing so you can become genuinely confident and at ease with yourself. I have no desire for you to become cocky – that's easy, just become a good actor. My wish for you is to become genuinely confident so that you are at ease with yourself and so that you feel happy in the knowledge that you have the power to be, do and have whatever you want. And you have. It's time to take back your power!

CHAPTER 1

The Truth behind Confidence

Let me ask you this, have you ever met a baby that was not confident in his or her ability to succeed? Have you ever met a baby that criticised themselves or second guessed their ability to be, do or have, whatever he or she wanted? I doubt it. I'm sure you'll agree that babies and children are confident that success is a given, that it is inevitable. They embrace challenges as they arise, without questioning or limiting their ability to succeed or feel good. However, as we become adults we criticise ourselves and convince ourselves that confidence and success are "things" that some people have or are born with and others don't, that some people are more capable, stronger and driven than others, that some people are just born lazy, that some people are born happy and relaxed and that some people are just destined to be shy and awkward, to live life in fear-mode and to play small. Now ask yourself this, if any human on this planet was to be surgically operated on, could the most expert of doctors locate "confidence" or "success" anywhere within their body, even if those "professionals" spent their entire lives trying to find them? Any ounce of common sense would tell us no. The truth is, confidence and success are not things, nor are they genetic, despite what you may have been led to believe. Confidence and success are not things that some people get and others don't. They don't exist as a concrete entity – period. Confidence is a *feeling,* a moment-to-moment emotion, and emotions are never constant, even if they feel that way. Success is a result of life balance, of being the best you can be, and that too is emotionally driven. You may feel a specific emotion frequently, and as a result that state can *appear* constant, but emotions and states are never constant. Emotions and states change all the time and they are influenced by many factors, some you may be aware of, and some may have passed you by without you even realising. Either way, you can be happy in the knowledge that no matter how unconfident or unsuccessful you think you are, you are in fact a normal perfectly functioning human being that has the ability to be as confident and successful as you want!

Having worked with thousands of people who all had "confidence" and "success" issues, and having felt that way myself, I have come to realise that we are in fact all born naturally confident and successful. We are born with a *knowing* that we are truly amazing. As children we get excited about showing people what new things we can say and do. Over time and through experience, repetitive negative thought and poor programming, we start to worry about what others think of us, we adopt the notion that we are not good enough, and shy away from situations where we might have to perform, be exposed, or be potentially judged. In a way we disown our authenticity and potential. Why do we do this? Why do we look down upon ourselves with such self-doubt, criticism and limiting beliefs, when the reality is each of us is amazing and we are all born capable of doing the most wonderful things – if we would stop buying into the notion that confidence and success are "things" we need to feel good and have a great life. It's about time to put things into perspective.

Environmental Programming

Imagine this scenario:

I bring you to a computer store to buy a computer. As we are browsing a sales assistant approaches us and asks us if we would like some help. We accept as we have no idea what to buy or how to use a computer. He goes on to explain which one he thinks we should buy. We are not knowledgeable about computers so we opt for the laptop he recommends. Picking it off the shelf, he asks if we want some extra programmes so we can do many things on the computer. Again, not knowing much about the products, we trust his judgment and buy the ones he recommends. He proceeds to set up an email account for us, just to be extra helpful. We are delighted with our purchase.

A little while later we decide to test out our new computer. We turn on the laptop and open the programmes. Feeling excited, we proceed to play around with programmes and we test our new email account. It's tricky at first but after an hour we learn how to navigate our way around. Over the next few months, using the computer every day, we become very good at using the programmes. A while later we can operate the programmes as easy as we can turn on a TV.

Now I want you to liken that computer experience to your brain. Just like going into the computer store, we are born into the world. Instead of getting a computer, we get a brain. Instead of computer programmes surrounding us, we get programmes (information) from other people and things - from our environment. The sales assistant could be likened to the people we meet in life, the people who were born into the world before us. Just as we trusted the sales assistant's recommendations, we trust the experts around us. After all, they have been here longer than us so they are more knowledgeable than we are. We accept what they say, we mimic what they do, and we follow instructions as they are given. With regular practice and over time we become good at what we are exposed to and at what we learn. For example, I was brought into the world of an English speaking family and I learned to speak English. I was exposed to it every day so I speak English fluently. My friend on the other hand was born into a French speaking family. Guess what she speaks? Yes, she speaks French. We learn what we are exposed to and we become good at what we repeat or practice, good or bad. And during our initial stages of life our programmes are for the most part chosen for us.

Since we were born and up to this moment we are receiving programmes every second. Some of the programmes are useful and some are not. Unfortunately, just as a computer cannot tell how useful a programme or email is until it is opened, our brains accept whatever they are presented with, good or bad, only to possibly filter later on. Don't think of a pink elephant. You thought of a pink elephant, didn't you? You see, our brains try on all information, not just some of it. It's then up to us to decide what to do with it. And just as a bad computer programme or virus-laden email would cause frustration, we often find ourselves frustrated when we don't operate effectively in our lives or businesses. We get upset when things don't turn out the way we want or when we behave in ways we don't like, sometimes not even knowing why we are that way. The reality is what we do is an imitation of, or a response to, something we were exposed to, everything from our accent and language to our state of mind and physical health. I refer to this programming process as *environmental programming*.

However, it's very important to understand that just because you may have been programmed a certain way it is not an excuse for not being, doing or having what you want in life going forward. We can always choose to let go of, or at least not operate from, programmes that no longer serve us and instead we can choose to learn and use new productive programmes, the same way that your current language does not impact your ability to learn another language. Change is possible at any time. We may have accepted the environmental junk we were fed but we are ultimately responsible for how our lives turn out from now on. And now is all we have. The past is gone and the future hasn't happened. It's time to take ownership for the results you want in your life from now on and let go of the things that don't serve you. If you want to feel confident and successful, you must be prepared to put aside the thoughts and behaviours that aren't useful. You must be prepared to let go of past hurts or "failings". Are you? Fortunately modern science has advanced enough that we can do this if you so choose to have a better life.

Using equipment such as PET (Positron emission tomography) scans, MRI (Magnetic Resonance Imaging) scans and EEGs (electroencephalograms) etc., we are now able to see how our brains behave and respond in various situations and to environmental stimuli. We can see how we accept information, how we deal with information and how we change information in our brains and bodies.

Our brains can do many things, which might make them seem complex, but the reality of it is our brains actually operate from very simplistic systems, many systems but simple ones nonetheless. Using technology we can see how these systems work and why they exist. We can literally train our brain for change! It's time to understand how your brain has been operating so we can update your programmes to more productive ones.

The Limbic System

We now know that the environmental programming process takes place for the most part in an area of the brain called the limbic system. This part of our brain is quite primitive (all animals have it) and it is also responsible for our automatic behaviours and habits and our emotional associations and responses. This would explain why certain songs or smells evoke certain emotions in us, even if the emotions are ones we don't like. If we experience a certain song, for example, on vacation or at a funeral, whatever emotion we experienced at the time will be attached to the song, and when the song is played in future (or a similar sounding one), the same emotions are triggered, almost instantly – a classic example of environmental programming in action. Isn't it true that the same song could trigger totally different emotions in someone who has a different association with the song? The association is what determines the response, not the song or situation itself.

Studies have shown that the limbic system area of the brain also finds it very difficult *on a neurological level* to tell the difference between what is happening in reality and what is happening in our imagination. It has been found that the brain engages the same neurological reactions, whether we are doing something for real or merely imagining doing it. These patterns are similar to small tracks engraved in the brain cells. So, if at some point in time we associated an intense emotion with a situation, stimulus or behaviour, as soon as we come in contact with the same or similar situation, stimulus or behaviour, the same emotions will be triggered. And the more we trigger that response, the stronger the programme gets. This is one reason why we might avoid doing things that on a logical level could benefit us, such as practising things that we want to become confident in or executing strategies for a successful outcome. Logically it may make sense that we should do certain things but if our emotional brain isn't on side, we don't do it.

Example: Anna found social interaction very

difficult. She felt comfortable in a one to one situation but when it came to group situations she felt terrified and avoided them at all costs. As a result, she became shy and turned down invitations to parties and events. Why? Aren't people in groups just a bunch of individuals grouped together? It's not like if an individual joins four others individuals they change or become dangerous because of it. Well the limbic system doesn't operate from logic; it operates from emotionally tagged programmes. You see, six years previously, Anna found herself being bullied by a group of people at work. Anna's "emotional brain" feared the same painful experience happening again. Although she wanted to attend parties and events, her emotionally tagged programme wouldn't let her. Our brains don't like pain of any kind! It was only when Anna let go of the emotion associated with the bullying at work that she could go on to feel comfortable in groups.

Programming and associations happen at a neurological level and because our brains operate at lightning speed we often don't consciously know why we do what we do. There are so many reasons for our behaviours and habits. For some it's being told they were stupid at school, for others it may be a brief comment about height, hair, voice or ability. It could be anything and you could drive yourself crazy trying to figure it out. The great thing is you don't need to figure it out to change or drop the programme!

The key to changing programmes, getting positive results and maintaining them, is not in analysing. In fact analysing often strengthens programmes. Changing programmes is achieved by changing *perspective,* intentionally changing how our brains *perceive* a situation or outcome and dealing with the associated emotion. You already know how you feel; analysing it will not change it. No matter how many times you analyse, you will not become confident by that alone. You cannot change the past but you can change perspective and by implementing specific strategies you can feel as confident as you want, and most importantly it will allow you to feel confident being *yourself.* If you get your brain to see that doing something feels good (like being confident or achieving successful outcomes), with the right action steps you will achieve what you want. In this book you will learn all of the steps you need. However, don't be surprised if your brain fights you before it allows the change!

The Habit of Resistance

Our brain's ability to automate responses is a brilliant system. We couldn't possibly learn and relearn everything all of the time as we process so much information every minute of the day. Our brains have to simplify matters and so they file information on a priority basis for automatic use. Habits are created this way. However, when we try to change habits our brains can become uncomfortable with the idea, even if the change will ultimately serve us better. We like the familiar. The *known* is easier and more comfortable. So, as you begin to change your programmes don't be surprised if your brain fights against it first. Our brains don't care if what we are used to is good or bad; routine and familiar programmes are preferred. Let's look at a simple example of this in action.

Example: Mandy drives home from work every evening after she clocks out at 5pm. She takes her usual route and stops off for her favourite chocolate bar on the way home. When she gets home she leaves her car keys on the table inside the door and proceeds into the kitchen, where she turns on the kettle to make a cup of tea – just in time for her favourite TV show. When the water is boiled she makes her tea in her favourite mug and proceeds into her living room. She sits on "her chair" and relaxes for the evening.

The above scenario is a typical after work evening for many people. Now imagine we change Mandy's routine. Instead of her usual routine, we get her to take an alternative route home from work, meaning she cannot stop for her chocolate bar. When she gets home she immediately goes to put her keys on the table but we have moved the table to a different room. We have also taken her favourite mug from her cupboard and when she goes into her living room she finds that her partner is sitting in her seat. Although these changes aren't exactly life threatening, they irritate and annoy Mandy. And they do for most of us. The fact is human beings like routine and the smallest of changes can frustrate us. However, if we understand that there could be possible discomfort before we make changes it makes those changes easier. Simply being aware of and acknowledging the fact is usually enough. The key is to be open and willing to change. And to do that we must look at how we currently perceive ourselves.

Your Identity

In an effort to help people understand who we are and why we do what we do, we adopt what are called identity labels, e.g. "I am a nurse", "I am a plumber", I am a worrier", "I am anxious", "I am depressed", "I am an introvert"," I am a failure", "I am stupid", "I am an awkward person" etc. Labels make it easy for our brains to understand and process lots of information quickly. This would be fine if that information was accurate and useful. However, it often isn't. The reason it isn't is that in order to create labels we have to nominalise our experiences and perceptions. This can be detrimental to our wellbeing. A nominalisation is when we use a noun (a thing) to describe a process, feeling or experience. For example, when someone calls themselves a "worrier" they are describing the process of feeling worried as a thing, not a feeling. They make the feeling of worry concrete. The problem with doing this is that it makes it a constant, which in turn packs it with all sorts of connotations and meanings. As a result we limit what we allow ourselves to do, be and have, and in some cases we use it as an excuse to get out of doing things that could ultimately be good for us. For example, "I'm a worrier so I need a private room to take an exam, in case I get a panic attack." or "I have depression so I can't do x, y or z.", when the reality might be "I am feeling scared and I don't know how to make myself feel relaxed in a room with other people." or "I often feel really low and I don't know how to change it." Identity labels can leave us disempowered, as though some thing is superior to us. I used to use identity labels that didn't serve me. In fact, I operated under one that nearly killed me! It is at this point that I will tell you how I know what it is to feel true pain and desperation. I know what it feels like to be utterly miserable and emotionally stuck. You see, when I was just twelve years old I was diagnosed with anorexia nervosa. Nobody, including myself, knew how to "cure" me. As a result, and feeling hopeless I stayed "anorexic" for years. My identity label was "I am anorexic" and it brought with it all kinds of difficulties. Eventually "anorexia" drove me into such a hole that I was given one week to live. That's how dangerous identity labels can be!

It was only when I took back my power by changing perspective that my life changed for the better. The reality was I was not Anorexia. I was (and am) Donna. I was simply choosing to engage in a very unproductive behaviour. For years I repeatedly chose to *do* anorexia. I didn't eat, I wouldn't eat, and I almost died as a result. However, having learned to think differently, "I changed my mind" and I now choose not to do anorexia behaviour. For the last seventeen years I have not engaged in anorexia behaviour whatsoever and I have no interest in doing so ever again. So what happened? Did, by some miracle, on the day I decided to change my behaviour, the monster "anorexia" just decide to up and leave me? Of course not, my choices changed and I let the *label* go. I decided that if I was to live a full productive and successful life, I had to let the anorexic label go. Don't get me wrong, I'm not naive enough to think that if you're finding things difficult, it's a matter of saying 'I don't want that behaviour anymore' and Abracadabra all is well. It takes time (less time than you might think) to train your brain for good behaviour but as soon as you make the decision to let the unproductive identity label go, life starts to change beautifully. Now think about this, in the next moment do you think I could choose to engage in anorexia behaviour again? Absolutely! I could make the choice right now not to eat again and go on to die a miserable death. But it's not the case that Anorexia would suddenly decide to get me again; it would be a matter of me making an unproductive decision and choosing to do the unproductive anorexia behaviour again. I could easily take on the "I am an anorexic" label. I choose not to. It's disempowering. I know that may seem like a blunt and possibly controversial thing for anyone to say but I guess I'm qualified to say it to you as I've lived it. I'm not just spouting text book material at you to make myself sound intelligent. I have lived through pain and come out the other side of it happy. To get you real results in the real world I will tell it to you as it is.

When we nominalise emotions we make doing what we want to do, be and have very challenging. If what we want does not fit within our existing identity label, by the very essence of the nominalisation, we cannot allow ourselves to do, be or have what we want. For example, "depressed, shy Mary" couldn't be seen to get excited and have fun. She's been "depressed, shy Mary" for years. Being happy would change her life dynamic.

Nominalised Confidence and Success

If you don't feel confident or successful, you have undoubtedly nominalised your emotions at some point in your life, either consciously or unconsciously, and what's more you, most likely unintentionally, allowed them to define you. When it comes to identity, saying I am or I have something is like slapping a massive sticker on your front and walking around with it for the whole world to see. "I am" and "I have" define you and they are very powerful definitions. What are your *current* "I am" and "I have" statements? How have you labelled yourself? Is it productive? I'd like you to grab a pen now and write them down in the space below so we can quickly begin to see what's happening for you. Writing things down will get you better results than just reading alone. Be totally honest with yourself, even if it's uncomfortable. I promise that doing this little exercise will serve you well. It's important at this stage that you do it, before reading on. You will see why later.

I am ____________________

I am ____________________

I am ____________________

I am ____________________

I am ____________________

I have ____________________

I have ____________________

I have ____________________

I have ____________________

I have ____________________

Now is the time to start to drop the unproductive nominalised statements. Take back your power by replacing your old "I am" and "I have" nominalised identity statements with positive productive "I am" and "I have" *descriptive choice statements*.

To help you do this I want you to think of the good things about you and turn them into *activity*. Write ten "I am" *descriptive choice statements*. For example,

I am choosing to be healthy

I am ______________________________

I am ______________________________

I am ______________________________

I am ______________________________

I am ______________________________

I am ______________________________

I am ______________________________

I am ______________________________

I am ______________________________

I am ______________________________

Labels and descriptions can make or break you. Be very careful which ones you use. Nothing is a permanent concrete entity, we "do" and we "feel" in moment-to-moment processes and experiences. If you want to do or feel something, all you need to do is engage in a process often. It's time to start doing things that take you in the confident, successful direction you want and deserve.

Be Authentic

I understand that it might feel somewhat daunting to put aside the identities and nominalisations that you or others have placed upon you over the years. After all, it is easier to be what we have known ourselves to be and to be what others have expected us to be, even if it's not desirable. However, you were not put on this planet to be someone else's version of you and you are not here to play small; you were born to be *you*, to be authentic and to be brilliant. If you live in congruence with who you really are, who you are underneath all the layers of past programming, conditioning and nominalisations, you will experience the feeling of confidence and success in abundance and it will happen a lot quicker than you think. Imagine knowing with certainty that you are a worthwhile person and feeling totally capable of achieving whatever it is you desire. How great will that be? You can and will feel this.

Getting in touch with your Authentic Self

Many experts will tell you that to really get in touch with your true authenticity it will take a long time and that you will need to go through a process of analysis, with the focus being finding *your inner child,* to embark on a long psychological journey of self discovery and searching, which can take many months or even years to complete, after which you may or may not be happy and may or may not get better results. The theory goes that connecting to this inner child will reveal everything you need to know about yourself to live an authentic successful life.

To be honest, it saddens me to know that so many people buy into the inner child concept as it is portrayed when in reality both you and I know that the only person who has an inner child is a pregnant woman. The fact is life is ticking away and I don't believe in wasting precious life moments when I know a method that works faster and the results are more positive and long lasting. I wholeheartedly respect anyone who tries to help another human being but the truth is you already know what you've been through in life and how you feel. You don't need a psychological operation to be made more aware of it. Learning how to live with authenticity is not dependent on finding an inner child and it does not have to take months or years to achieve. The best way to understand who you are in an authentic state is to simply look at your *core values,* to identify what is truly important to you at the core and to live from that. Core values filter through everything and throughout your life, as you will soon see.

Values are the links and programmes that tie together personal perceptions and judgements, motives and actions. They are keys to understanding the reality behind your persona. And unless you live in congruence with your core values you will never feel authentic or confident and you will always feel that something isn't quite right in your life. A conflict in core values can be responsible for anything from feeling confident to a poor relationship or even an argument. If your current behaviours and feelings are not ones that you like then you are certainly not living in accordance with your core values. Have a look at some core values in the box below. Then I want you to answer the two questions opposite.

INTEGRITY	HELPING	RESPONSIBILITY
HEALTH	FORGIVENESS	RESOURCEFULNESS
SELF-KNOWLEDGE	COMPASSION	SELF-HELP
HONESTY	WEALTH	DISCIPLINE
REASON	INNER CALM	DOING GOOD
INTEREST	FAMILY	SECURITY
REFLECTION	SELF-RESPECT	COOPERATION
FRANKNESS	CONTENTMENT	SOLIDARITY
RESPECT FOR LIFE	SELF-CONTROL	UNITY
LOVE	INDEPENDENCE	NON-VIOLENCE
GIVING	TEMPERANCE	LAWFULNESS
SHARING	FREEDOM	SOCIAL SERVICE
KINDNESS	EQUALITY	GENTLENESS
RELATIONSHIP	HELPFULNESS	COURTESY
CONCERN	RESPECT	SPIRITUALITY

1) What matters most to you in life?

2) What behaviours do others have that irritate or annoy you most?

The truth is, when your core values are being compromised, either by yourself, someone else or a situation, you will know all about it! Your mood, your relationships, your behaviour - they are all linked to your core values. For example, if honesty is one of your core values and you are in a work environment that requires you to be dishonest, how calm or authentic do you think you would feel? Not very. Do you think you would be unsettled, upset, irritable, or grumpy? You bet you would! You need to bring things back to basics. Simplify. If something is important to you, make it important. Be YOU! Live from your core values.

Tapping Into Your Authenticity

Close your eyes for a few moments and vividly imagine what you would be like if you felt more at ease with yourself than you have been feeling.

Move your body now into the exact posture you would be in if you felt truly authentic, confident and successful.

Imagine in detail how you would think and behave and how you would speak to yourself. Feel it. Connect with it.

CHAPTER 2

Creating a Solid Foundation

Everything worthwhile is built on a solid foundation. If we are to create a more confident successful you, we need to build a solid authentic foundation for you first, with congruent core values and balance. If we do not, the confidence and success you feel will only be brief. Not only that, in times of environmental stress, which everyone experiences at various points in life, having a solid authentic foundation will allow you to remain sturdy and focused on living life fully and achieving what you want, no matter what life may bring or how possible you think something is or isn't. Life events happen that we can do nothing about but it's not situations that will determine who you become; it's how you respond to them that makes the difference. It's what we do with what happens to us that matters. A solid foundation puts you in a very strong position to deal with whatever happens in your life. In fact I would go so far as to say it is essential to everything you do from now on. Your level of life balance determines your results.

Now

In order for us to build the foundation we need to look at what we're working with at this point in time. If it's good, bad or chaotic, it doesn't matter. We will work with your life as it is *now* so we get the best results for you going forward. The exercise below is designed to identify your *starting point*. It is straightforward but not necessarily easy as it requires you to be one hundred percent honest with yourself. It is not an exercise in criticism of any kind. Its purpose is purely to acknowledge what is currently happening in your life right now and that is all. It is *essential* that you do this exercise at this stage. Once completed, and once you start to implement the strategies throughout this book, you will begin to see how important this foundation is.

Step 1

Read the list of needs that I have outlined in the next six pages and ask yourself how each need applies to you and your life right now. Ask yourself if each need listed is being met in balance in your life at the moment and give yourself a score between 1 and 10. Please note that most people do not have their needs met in balance (many don't even know what their needs are) so don't worry if, when you identify and rate your needs, things look awful. Nobody scores a ten on everything, if anything, but rating your situation in this way will help you identify what specifically needs to change and/or improve so you feel most confident and get best results.

Physical needs

Our physical needs are perhaps the most obvious to us but I will detail them here so you are confident that your baseline needs are met. They are the basis of human survival and it's important they are met in balance if we are to get optimal results. Compromising your physical needs can make balancing your emotional needs more difficult. For example, if you don't have good nutrition, like I hadn't, your ability to think clearly will be significantly affected. This in turn can affect everything else. Get the basics right and build on that.

Shelter

- Having a roof over our heads is something so many of us take for granted but when it is taken away from you it can have a huge impact on your sense of confidence and self worth. Being homeless or living in poor conditions can be enough to make anyone feel bad and it can impair your ability to progress in other areas. If you don't have a roof over your head, it is vital that you seek assistance as soon as possible. There is no shame in asking for help!

Score (1-10): ☐

Fresh Air

- Our brains require a constant flow of oxygen to function normally so it's important to get lots of fresh air every day. It will allow you to function at your best. It will allow your "happy hormones" to kick in.

Score (1-10): ☐

Good Nutrition

- Good nutrition is essential to a confident you. In particular, the B group vitamins, especially B5 and B6, are very important for mood and hormone balance. Omega-3 fatty acids are also excellent for optimal brain function. They have been shown to improve focus, attention span and concentration.

Score (1-10): ☐

Clean Water

- Next to oxygen, clean water is the most essential element to human life; the body usually cannot survive longer than several days without water (a maximum of 1 week). Water is essential to the functioning of every single cell and organ system in your body and makes up greater than 2/3 of the weight of the human body; the brain is 75% water, blood is 83% water, bones are 22% water, muscles are 75% water, and the lungs are 90% water. It is needed for the efficient elimination of waste products through the kidneys, regulation of body temperature (through perspiration), cushioning for the joints, good digestion and metabolism, delivery of nutrients and oxygen to all cells in the body and it facilitates all of the chemical processes which occur in the body. Without water we would die. And a decrease of as little as 2% in our body's water supply can have harmful effects and cause symptoms of dehydration, such as daytime fatigue, excess thirst, fuzzy memory, difficulty focusing on tasks, feeling lightheaded, and nausea. This can all affect your motivation to get better results.

For optimal body function, look into getting a water filter that alkalises your water. It will allow your body to be in its best state.

Score (1-10): ☐

Sleep

- We need sleep to function properly. If we do not get enough sleep it can have effects on both our mental and physical health, which will affect how confident you feel. Aim for seven to eight hours sleep every night. There are several studies that show people who get inadequate sleep have poorer performance than people who get enough sleep. Just like a computer, your brain needs time to recharge.

Score (1-10): ☐

Movement and Muscle

- Regular physical activity is one of the most important things we can do for our bodies and our brains. Movement releases endorphins, also known as happy hormones.

Score (1-10): ☐

Emotional Needs

Most people don't even know what their emotional needs are, never mind take care of them. However, ignoring or compromising your emotional needs is what causes most people's problems and without question determines how confident you will feel and what results you achieve. It is very important to review how balanced your emotional needs are.

Safety and Security

- In general, we feel safe when we feel competent to deal with whatever is happening in our lives and we feel secure when we know that our environment (emotional, financial etc.) is stable. Feeling insecure and unsafe is very common as life is so unpredictable. If we experience life challenges, it can really ruffle our sense of safety and security, leaving us fearing the unknown, which is perhaps the scariest feeling known to human beings. It's important to create a solid foundation.

Score (1-10): ☐

Control

- Every human being needs to have a sense of order and control in life, whether that is in deciding what to wear or planning the future. However, sometimes we can experience situations that cause us to feel helpless, such as family illness or job uncertainty, which can affect how confident we feel.

  The aim is to create calm amongst any chaos.

Score (1-10): ☐

Competency and Achievement

- Feeling proud of ourselves, feeling "good enough" is very important to our emotional wellbeing. Unfortunately, as stated earlier, in today's fast paced society, we so often measure ourselves against other people. The house we own, the car we drive, the relationship we are in, how we look, how we perform etc. We've become a society of comparisons, instead of acknowledging our competency and ability.

Score (1-10): ☐

Attention (to give and receive)

- Attention, both giving it (contribution to others) and receiving it, is essential to development and emotional wellbeing. Everyone needs a sense of inclusion and appreciation, to feel their presence has been noted.

Score (1-10): ☐

Connection to others

- Our brains are social organs; in the womb, neurons in the developing brain become functional only if they connect with other neurons, implying it is in our make up to interact and be part of something. It is natural (and important) to need other people in our lives.

Score (1-10): ☐

Purpose and Meaning

- Countless studies have shown that having a strong sense of purpose in life is associated with greater overall mental health, happiness, and even longevity. It's important that we have something to get up for, to have something that stretches our mind and body or something we can look forward to doing. That could be anything from being part of a class to learning something new at home. Stimulate your brain!

Score (1-10): ☐

Fun and Relaxation

- Life without fun and relaxation can easily become meaningless. The human mind and body cannot go through life in a constant flow of adrenaline, the same way a car cannot run forever without a fuel injection. We must have down time, time to recharge and recoup.

Score (1-10): ☐

Love and Affection

- Everyone needs to feel loved and cared for, whether that is from a partner, a child or a pet. I guess it's the world's way of saying we are worthwhile. This love and affection can be as simple as a hug or cuddle, a feeling of having a bond with something other than ourselves.

Score (1-10): ☐

Step 2

Now I want you to rate your current situation, in terms of balance as outlined in Step 1. I'd like you to shade in each area of the wheel below, which will

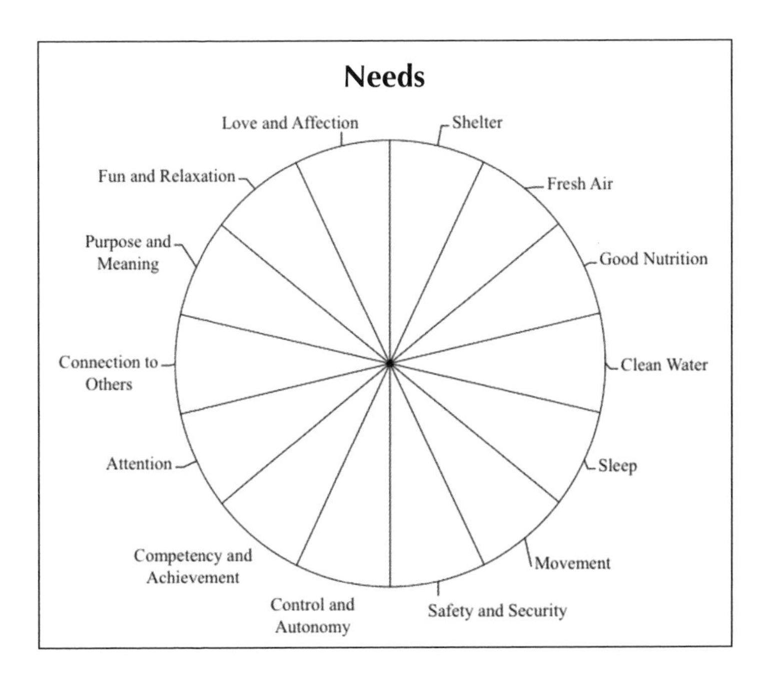

graphically represent how balanced your needs are on a scale of 1-10. A score 1 is the inner most point and 10 is the outer edge of the circle. If you feel a need is totally balanced it would score a 10. If a need is totally imbalanced it would score a 1. And if a need is average it would score 5 and so on. A score of 10 does not mean perfection in general terms, it simply defines *your ideal* in that area. For example, my 10 in physical health is not to be an athlete, yet for someone else it might be. Define your 10 and then rate where you are currently. We want a graphic representation of what your life looks like right now so we can measure your progress as we go along.

So, how did you score – disaster? Relax! Most people's needs wheel looks shabby. When I first did this exercise my wheel looked horrendous. But can you imagine if that wheel was on your car? How bumpy would the ride be? Getting your needs fulfilled in a balanced healthy way is essential to your success and how you feel!

Filling the Gap

It is human nature to want to fill gaps. For example, when we see an open space on a wall we feel obliged to hang a picture, just so it doesn't look like something's missing. It is in our nature to seek completion. When it comes to human needs, we seek that same completion. We look for balance and fulfilment. However, in many cases we don't know how to fulfil our needs. For example, when I experienced signicant personal challenges in my own life, my sense of control and security was very imbalanced. I didn't feel I had any. What's more, I didn't know how to get back that sense of control and security. As a result, I engaged in controlling behaviour (anorexia behaviour) in an attempt to fill the gap. We can fill that gap productively or unproductively, depending on what seems easiest or most effective at the time. The extremity of the behaviour and associated feelings are determined by how balanced or imbalanced a need is.

You could liken it to a plant trying to get its needs met. A plant needs certain things in balance to bloom. It needs water, sunlight, oxygen, etc. But what would happen if we deprived the plant of water, for example? It would die, right? Possibly but not before it gives its best attempt to get its need met. It might plunge its roots down in any direction in search of water and it might strip water from its leaves –anything in an attempt to meet the need.

We are the same. If our needs are unmet we will do everything we can to get them met, even if we look and feel miserable in the process. Over indulging in alcohol or drugs, overeating, under-eating, criticising, bullying, promiscuity, withdrawing from society, etc. – there are so many ways we, as humans, try to get our needs met, sometimes productively and sometimes unproductively. Your current behaviour and associated feelings are a reflection of your needs-balance as it exists right now. Think about it, what are you doing too much of or too little of that isn't productive and that you might like to change? How does that behaviour make you feel? Look at the wheel you just filled in. That unproductive behaviour will have a compensatory link to one or more of the needs you scored lowest on your wheel.

Our behaviour and feelings relate to how well our needs are being met at any given time. If you are indulging in a behaviour that isn't useful, especially if you are doing it often, your brain is trying to fill the gap of an unmet need. The behaviour serves a purpose. By completing your needs wheel it will quickly become apparent to you what those unmet needs are. The key is to then look for ways to create healthy balance. As your needs wheel becomes more balanced, the behaviour you don't want will naturally stop as your brain has no further use for it. Not only that, you will begin to feel better and behave more productively. Start creating balance in your life today by taking a small step each day and every day. Think about this, if you make just a 1% improvement each day on a consistent basis, which is doable, at the end of the year you will be 365% better than you are now! And this brings us to the third step in this exercise.

Step 3

In the spaces below, write a *1% Improvement Action Step* that you can take *today* to get your needs more in balance. I will help you with this throughout the book but for now write down a simple step you can implement today to make a difference, no matter how small you think it is. For example, you might decide to practice the social skills you will learn later in this book, you might give yourself a half an hour quite time or you may be you could meet a friend. Whatever it is, write it down.

1% Improvement Action Step

Balancing Physical Needs

____

____

____

____

____

____

____

____

____

Balancing Emotional Needs

Safety and Security

Control and Autonomy

Competency and Achievement

Attention (to give and receive)

Connection to Others

Purpose and Meaning

Fun and Relaxation

Love and Affection

____

____

____

____

____

Ask!

At times everyone needs a little help getting their needs balanced. There is no shame in trying to improve your life and people are generally happy to help you to do it – if you ask them! People cannot help you if you don't tell them what you need. The truth is it's not other people's job to notice how well met your needs are. They have their own needs to be taking care of. It doesn't mean they don't care, it simply may mean that they don't realise you need help or it may not be something that would interest them personally, and that is okay. Everyone has different values and things that matter to them. It doesn't mean that what is important to you isn't important. Sometimes people just don't get it or even know what's going on. That said, it is important that you let people (or one person) know what's happening. If, for example, you need someone to help you interact more with people, ask them to accompany you to a social occasion. I used to ask my sister to bring me to cafés so I could get used to having people around me. I felt so insecure that I was afraid to sit in a cafe on my own. Having her there was a helpful start.

It's okay to ask for help

When I was in the midst of emotional challenge I had no desire or inclination to ask people to help me. I didn't know what my needs were or how to get them met and so I just thought my behavior was part of me. I was completely self-focused and wouldn't allow people in. In hindsight and now understanding human needs, I know that my being self-focused was required to allow me to continue the behavior and thus control my situation. At the time I didn't think I deserved to be happy and to give up the controlling behavior brought with it the possibility of being happy. I know it sounds crazy but a part of me didn't want to feel happy and I didn't feel I deserved to be happy. I just couldn't see anything good in my life to be happy about and I didn't want anyone to help me and take "my control" away from me. To be honest, my attitude to asking for help stank. I hated everything, mostly myself. I saw asking for help as some kind of weakness that would make me vulnerable.

However, with time I knew something had to change. I needed to ask for help. Although help had been offered many times, I had refused to accept it.

I had become so used to living the way I was, I had no idea how to change it. I was familiar with, but miserable in, my feelings at that time. Reluctantly, it came to a point where I had to admit that I wanted to get out of the state I was in, but I didn't know how and that I needed help.

The first person I truly asked for help from was my mother. I had just come out of a short coma and I remember crying and begging her to give me some direction. Her response was the turning point in my life. She looked at me with loving eyes and said *'Donna, I haven't known how to help you so I prayed about it. We need to look at what you can be grateful for.'* Well, I could have hit her! Grateful – what did I have to be grateful for?! Was she not getting the fact that my life was awful and I had no confidence to do anything? The last thing I needed to hear was that I should be grateful! What on earth was she telling me to be grateful for? I felt totally patronized. *"Be grateful"* – that's what's said to a child when they don't get what they want. I was irate. However, I relented. I had no option for recovery other than to trust her. We began writing things I could be grateful for. Well, she wrote for me as I was too weak. To be honest, at the beginning I couldn't think of anything to be grateful for. I hated my life. So she encouraged me by pointing out that I had hands and then that I could draw well. It took writing thirty nine things before I got a genuine smile on my face! I don't think even she knew how powerful that exercise was. It changed my life. To rise from distress, I had to acknowledge what I already had. I needed to adopt a new perspective, firstly an attitude of gratitude.

Whether you like it or not and whether you want to hear it or not, our attitude determines how successful we become. You will soon see what I mean and how you can use this to your advantage.

CHAPTER 3

Attitude

"No one can make you feel inferior without your consent."

– Eleanor Roosevelt

It's easy to notice the things that are wrong with our lives. We get used to life as we know it, rehashing all the bad stuff in the process. But if we spend all your time focusing on what's wrong and what's not working in our life, it's very difficult to notice what's going right for us. No matter what is happening in your life right now (and there are things going right for you), it's a matter of consciously stopping to listen and notice, to look for even the tiniest thing you can appreciate. This will open your mind to the *possibility* of a great life.

It was only when I consciously decided to adopt an attitude of gratitude that my approach to life as it was, changed dramatically! Gratitude gave me the start on which I could build my foundation for success. I believe it to be a two-part process:

1) **Let go Comparisons**.

2) **Acknowledge the things that you can be grateful for right now.** The fact you can read this sentence is a good place to start.

Comparisons

Comparing yourself to others can have a seriously damaging affect on how you feel and indeed on your results in both life and business. It can lead to a feeling of inadequacy, jealousy and even resentment, all of which drown any opportunity to feel confident or successful. It's unfortunate considering that our perception of other people's circumstances is usually so inaccurate. Trust me, very few people have the life you think they have. Portrayal is often very different to reality. I don't know anyone who has a perfect life and I know a lot of apparently "perfect" people. We all have hiccups and things that aren't exactly as we would like. Let's be real here. If you are focused on what others have and what you don't have, it makes it very difficult to get where you want to go. It prevents you from seeing the great things you have in your life already. To demonstrate this to you I'd like you to do this little exercise:

Become aware of where you are right now. If you're indoors notice the furniture around you, the walls, the light fitting etc. If you're outside notice the trees, the flowers and whatever else surrounds you. Now list the items you see that are brown in color.

Brown Items

____

____

____

____

____

____

When you have listed them, close your eyes and without opening them, try to recall all the black items around you.

Did you find it more difficult to recall the black items?

The point is that our brain only allows us to consciously process five to nine pieces of information at any one time – the things we place priority on – and it filters out the rest. That being the case, if you are comparing yourself to others and think you are, or have, less than they have, that is exactly what your brain will notice, whether it is the case in reality or not. It will prioritize lack, not abundance. Have you ever decided to buy a new car and all of a sudden that car type seemed to be everywhere, and you started to notice more car adverts? We see what we place most focus on. Now it's time to focus on how wonderful you really are and how much you have in your life. It's time to wake up.

If you make a conscious decision to notice good things about you and your life, and be grateful for them, you will be very surprised at how quickly life feels so much better and how you seem to get so much more. I call this the Law of *Conscious Detection*. It's a matter of deciding how you want to feel and what you want in your life, placing conscious priority on it, and letting your brain detect it for you! Our lives are a reflection of how we think, how we perceive events and circumstances, and ultimately what we choose to focus on, past, present and future. If you want to feel more confident, you need to consciously decide to focus on the good things about YOU and YOUR life. Notice your good qualities, your strengths, your resources, your talents, the little things in life, like when you receive a compliment or a smile. Give your brain instruction as to what you want it to notice and remind it often. This is why visualization works so well; it is clearly telling your brain what to look for and what to see more of. This is also why affirmations help; they are frequent reminders of what to focus on. Fill your environment with prompts to help you notice the good things in your life and the good things about you. For example, I put visual prompts on my phone and computer screen saver. Every time I open them, I am reminded to focus on positive things and on my goals. You could put a little note on the dashboard of your car or on your fridge, somewhere you will be reminded often.

Acknowledging the things you can be grateful for right now

The second part to having an attitude of gratitude is to use a Gratitude Journal. Every night before you go to sleep write down ten things you can be grateful for that day in your journal. Not only will this end your day on a high, it will prepare your brain for programming positive programs while you sleep. You can also do this first thing in the morning before you get out of bed. Let's give you a practice run now. List ten things below that you are grateful for. I'll start you off...

1) *I am grateful for my eyes.*

2) *I am grateful I can read this book.*

3) ______________________________

4) ______________________________

5) ______________________________

6) ______________________________

7) ______________________________

8) ______________________________

9) ______________________________

10)______________________________

If you are to achieve anything worthwhile in life, you need to adopt the right attitude. It will help you feel how you want to feel and get what you want faster. All too often we focus on our past "failings", our mistakes and our regrets. We dwell on what we did wrong and what we should have done differently or we blame others for how we are, how we feel and for what we do. None of that is productive to a good life and it will keep us stuck. Not only that, it will make us bitter. The only way we will get what we want is to focus on what *is* good in our life, even if we think that's not a lot, and then we need to build on that. I'm not suggesting that you dismiss anything bad that happened in your life, but I am saying that dwelling on those bad things and allowing them to keep you stuck won't do you any favours or bring you to a better place. To move beyond all the negative stuff a change in attitude is required and that is a *choice*. I don't want to sound patronizing when I say attitude is a choice, but it is! I've been in emotional hell, as I said, so I'm qualified to say it as it is. My aim here is to help you move out of the state you don't want, not wrap you in cotton wool. Unfortunately, that means hearing some things you might not like. The concept of attitude being a choice was a hard fact for me to accept but when I did, I became happier and I made much better choices. Attitude is a moment-to-moment choice, as you will soon see. Today do yourself a valuable favour and make a choice to consciously focus only on the good things in your life, not on the bad stuff you may have been dwelling on. Acknowledge the bad stuff for what it was and let it go now, focusing on it does not serve you. Instead, focus on what you *do* want. You must give your brain something good to work with. Let's start by looking at what you have already achieved. Let's look at your successes.

Look at what you've already achieved!

Whether you realise it or not you have achieved so many things in your life already. You already have the ability to be successful. You are capable! You don't have to have climbed Mount Everest or to have seen the wonders of the world to have achieved something worthwhile. It's easy to cast your achievements aside, as though they don't matter – but they do matter! You matter.

You are worthwhile and your accomplishments deserve recognition. I'd like you now to list 20 of your life successes. Remind yourself of your triumphs. Start when you were very young and think of all your achievements since then. Don't just pick the big things, write down all the things you may have taken for granted. Things like learning to talk, learning to ride a bike, getting your spellings right, getting your first job, being involved in a fund-raising campaign etc. Reflect back on your "I am" descriptive statements in Chapter 1 as they can help you remember the things you have achieved so far. For example, if you are reading this book you have mastered reading so you would write, *I am good at reading*. Do you realise how difficult it is to learn to read when you don't know how to? You may have forgotten but ask any adult that doesn't know how to read how difficult it is. Be confident in the fact that you are a capable competent human being and never take your brilliance for granted. Yes, you are brilliant!

Things I have already achieved

1) ______________________________

2) ______________________________

3) ______________________________

4) ______________________________

5) ______________________________

6) ______________________________

7) ______________________________

8) ______________________________

9) ______________________________

10) ______________________________

11) ______________________________

12) ______________________________

13) ______________________________

14) ______________________________

15) ______________________________

16) ______________________________

17) ______________________________

18) ______________________________

19) ______________________________

20) ______________________________

If you have reached 20, feel free to write more if you like!

Taking it a step further...

To help you really focus on your successes, create a "Victory Log", in which you will list your daily successes, and review it anytime you are faced with a new challenge. By writing down your victories every day you're securing your competency in your long-term memory, which enhances your self-esteem and builds a feeling of certain confidence. It sets you on course for results! Your brain and your neurology will respond positively to your instruction and it will show you that you are actually more successful and capable than you may once have thought.

Identify Your Strengths

As we live our lives and experience criticism from others (and from ourselves), it is common to forget our strengths that, if tapped into, can help us to achieve whatever we want and be and feel however we want. You have developed strengths over time (strengths you may have taken for granted) that will be invaluable to you if you identify and acknowledge them and draw upon them as needed. Strengths can include anything from a personal characteristic to a skill or ability. For example, two of my strengths are my determination and discipline. In the past I used these strengths negatively to fuel anorexia behaviour. I was determined to destroy myself and disciplined enough to do it, but having made more useful choices since, I have chosen to channel that same determination and discipline for good outcomes. This is what has helped me get to where I am today. In fact it played a big part in making this book possible. I channel my strengths positively and you can too. Turn anything that seems like a weakness into strength!

It's really a matter of identifying where we have most

power and channelling it in a useful way for productive results. You can do this! I'd like you to identify your strengths here also and once you have done so, think about how you could channel them to help you get the positive results you want and deserve. An easy way to do this is to think about a past result (good or bad) and ask yourself what you needed to do and how you needed to be and feel to get that result. For example, it may have required you to be dedicated, loyal, kind, stubborn, focused or something else. Look at what emotion you put behind your result to get it.

Five strengths I recognise in myself

1) ______________________________

2) ______________________________

3) ______________________________

4) ______________________________

5) ______________________________

Q. How can I use the above in a positive way to get me the results I want?

____

____

____

____

Identify Your Resources

Make a list of every person and thing in your life that you can draw upon as a resource to bring you toward the results that you want. This might include family, friends, colleagues, contacts, groups in the community, classes, finance, personal talents, knowledge, skills or abilities, books etc. List everything you can think of that you can draw upon. When you take the time to think about your resources you might find that you have more to help you than you thought.

My Resources

The key to becoming a more confident you, is to tap into what is natural to you and use it for good. Channel it in the right direction. Before reading the next chapter, fill in the exercises outlined thus far and think about how you can use all you've identified to enhance your life. I know it may seem like a bit of work but it will be worth it, I promise! The purpose of this book is to get you results, not just entertain you. Take a few moments before reading on. Think of your desired outcomes and about how good you will feel living your life. Now let's get your mind and body working together so we can enhance, ensure and make feeling confident and successful automatic!

CHAPTER 4

The Mind Body Link

In 1946 Norbert Weiner, a professor of mathematics at the Massachusetts Institute of Technology, coined a term *cybernetic loop*. Fancy name aside, it refers to mechanical systems that regulate themselves. For example, your refrigerator's temperature is controlled using a cybernetic loop device. As the temperature rises, the thermostat turns on a motor that runs a compressor that cools the interior. When the interior reaches the correct temperature, the thermostat turns off the motor – a perfect synergistic relationship in action. Our minds and bodies work on a similar system called a *psycho- cybernetic loop*. In a nutshell it means that whatever you think about will affect the way your body responds and whatever way you use your body will affect how you think. Remember, how you think determines your ability to succeed!

It's not rocket science when you think of it in the context of people you know. Think about someone you know who feels unhappy and shy. You will notice that their movements are slower than normal, that they slump and look down instead of straight ahead, and that their breathing is slow and shallow. Now think of someone you know who feels confident and successful. Notice how they stand tall in a relaxed manner, how they look up and out instead of down, how they sit upright and their movements are self assured and strong. Now let me ask you this, what do you think would happen if we made an intentional shift in the physical posture of a person who feels unhappy, purposely ensuring they maintain a positive confident posture? On the flip side, what do you think would happen if we took a person who feels confident and asked them to purposely maintain an unhappy tired posture? Do you think their mood would change simply by a posture shift? Yes! I know, it seems almost too simple but think about it, anything that works well usually is a simple system. The fact is your mind and body always have to operate together never independently, the same as a refrigerator's temperature regulator. If you don't believe me try it for yourself. Slouch, pout a sad face, look down and make your breathing more shallow and slow. At the same time, *without* changing that posture, try to feel upbeat and happy. Maintain the unhappy posture for five minutes and you will notice you begin to feel depressed. I bet it won't even take five minutes! Try the opposite posture. Stand tall on purpose, shoulders back, chest out, and look straight ahead (slightly above eye level) with an intentional smile of pride on your face. Smile on purpose. At the same time, *without* changing that strong positive posture, try to feel depressed. It's very difficult to do! You will notice that in order to put yourself in a depressed state your brain naturally starts to shift to a depressed posture. The fact is the nature of the psycho-cybernetic loop makes it impossible to mismatch a posture and a feeling. If you adopt a posture of someone who looks depressed or even tired, you will start to feel that way at that moment. The more you stay in that posture, the more depressed and tired you will get. However, if you stand or sit with a confident successful posture you will start to feel confident and successful. And the more you do it and the more often you do it,the more confident you will feel, which in turn allows you to think successfully. It's the way the loop operates. Try it when you're speaking to someone on the phone, speak as though you are already super confident and successful. You will find that your tone of voice even picks up! Make your positive posture an automatic habit by doing it often – on purpose!

How does this happen?

In our bodies we have lots of chemicals, enzymes and hormones. Every time we do something those chemicals, enzymes and hormones activate or change. If we laugh, if we cry, if we move, if we eat, if we jog, if we drink something, if we experience temperature shifts, if we see someone we like or dislike, if we hear a sound, if we taste or smell something – the list could go on forever. The bottom line is everything we do every moment of our lives causes a chemical, enzyme and or hormonal change in our bodies. These changes are never constant, they go up and down all the time, and depending on what chemicals, enzymes and hormones are being activated at any given moment will determine the feelings and thoughts experienced. If you experience something bad in your life the cybernetic loop simply kicks in and triggers the corresponding chemicals, enzymes and hormones in that moment, resulting in you feeling upset or depressed, for example, the same way the refrigerator cooler kicks in to regulate temperature. This is why nominalising emotions is not smart. Our emotions are constantly being changed and regulated moment to moment, they are not constant.

If a bad situation continues, or if you do not deal with it, the same chemicals, enzymes and hormones activate over and over. This happens not because you contract some kind of concrete constant "incurable chemical imbalance" but because you either continue to experience the same situation in reality or because you are regularly thinking about it in your mind (mental rehearsal). Remember, our brains cannot (on an emotional and programming level) tell the difference between what is happening for real and what is happening in our minds. If we continue to rehash situations in our minds (good or bad) the associated chemicals, enzymes and hormones activate in the same way as they would if it was happening for real. So this being the case, it is so easy to nominalise emotions because they *seem* constant. Frequent activation of chemicals, enzymes and hormones can make things seem constant. You may have heard that people who "have" depression have chemical imbalances. In a way this is correct but only in the sense that they have not dealt with or are still experiencing a situation that is causing their chemicals, enzymes and hormones to activate frequently.

However, if the condition is *concrete and incurable,* which many people are led to believe it is, how is it then that it is possible to feel good after the events that caused the depressed state in the first place are dealt with? If it was a concrete condition, no matter what treatment was received, and no matter how much one tried, it would never get better. The key here is to become a victor, not a victim. Take control of what is happening in your life and work with, and not against, your mind and body naturally. You are in control – take control! You have the power to feel confident and to succeed in whatever way you want.

The 48 Hour Shake Up

For the next 48 hours, I want you to do a two step exercise to shake up your current thinking and behaviour.

1. Sit, move, talk and walk as though you feel totally confident and self assured. Think of what you would be as a totally confident person and act that way. If you find yourself slipping into your old posture, pull yourself up again. By doing this posture shift, your brain will receive new "updated" programmes and it will start to activate positive chemicals, hormones and enzymes to make your new confident posture comfortable and habitual for you.

2. Refrain from saying anything negative to yourself or about anyone else, whether that is in your mind or aloud. Keep all thoughts and words entirely positive. To make this easier I want you to place an elastic band on your wrist and if you find yourself engaging in anything negative snap the band on your wrist. Do this every time you think anything negative. Your brain will soon begin to change its old bad habit of thinking and behaving negatively!

Do this for a full 48 hours and watch what happens!

Working with your body and mind

Understanding the psycho-cybernetic loop and making changes to old programs or patterns of behaviour will help you manage your emotional states. However, there are some other important factors to consider when understanding the mind-body link so you can really use it to your optimal advantage. This will allow us to put you in the best position for positive change.

Serotonin

Serotonin is the key brain chemical that generates positive feelings, including feelings of confidence and optimism. Additionally, serotonin plays a role in certain brain functions such as the ability to focus, motor coordination, reflexes and hunger. As you would expect, when we lack sufficient serotonin a wide range of symptoms appear including a feeling of low self esteem, depression, edginess and negativity. Insomnia and poor concentration can also result. Our serotonin level, as any other chemical produced by our body, fluctuates moment to moment depending on what's happening in our environment (including our thoughts) and depending on what we are doing (or not doing) at the time, internally or externally. There's not a human being on the planet that has *constant* high or low serotonin levels, despite what chemists might have you believe.

Chemists have simply created a synthetic form of

the chemical and readily sell it as a solution to treating certain "conditions" that some people "have", such as anxiety, depression and sleep disorders. However, although the synthetic drug may give a temporary "lift" and will no doubt make chemists lots of money, doesn't it make more sense to find out why natural serotonin levels have decreased in the first place and sort the issue out naturally so it can be maintained long term, especially considering we can increase serotonin naturally? Yes you read it right we can increase our serotonin naturally! The only reason people don't do it, in my opinion, is because they don't know they can do it or they don't know how to do it.

Diet

- *Tryptophan*

  It is quite common for people to recommend eating foods that produce serotonin. On the surface that makes sense. If you need serotonin and specific foods contain it, why not just eat them? The problem is research indicates that eating serotonin found in food is rather pointless. Serotonin from food does not cross the blood-brain barrier, which means it has no effect on brain serotonin levels. So, it's not just a matter of eating foods that contain serotonin. However, eating protein-rich foods high in an amino acid called tryptophan, (the precursor to serotonin) *in combination with* a certain kind of carbohydrate has been found to increase serotonin levels in the brain. Natural food source tryptophan does not exist in isolation. Tryptophan belongs to the family of amino acids all of which bind together to form proteins. The carbohydrate is essential in that it stimulates serum insulin which, when it is released into the bloodstream, suppresses all amino acid levels, except for tryptophan. The body recognizes and readily absorbs this food solution and when tested clinically it has proved more effective than the drug form of tryptophan, without the risk of adverse side effects.

To be effective, the carbohydrate you eat must be a high-glycemic carbohydrate in order to induce enough of an insulin spike to draw the other amino acids away from the transport sites. However, the majority of your daily food should consist of low-glycemic foods, as importantly they keep your sugar levels constant throughout the day, preventing dips in energy levels, but for the purposes of increasing serotonin you could have a snack made up of a protein rich food and a high glycemic carbohydrate, ideally eaten after exercise. Examples of high glycemix index foods include cocoa (70% cocoa dark chocolate) rice, sweet fruits like pineapple, melon, banana or dates, mashed potatoes, cereals, bread and pasta. Examples of proteins include poultry, fish, dairy, soy, pumpkin seeds, sunflower seeds, cashew nuts, peanuts, almonds, walnuts, beans, split peas, and lentils. Simply mix and match! A fruit smoothie containing whey protein and seeds is a really easy option for a tryptophan boosting protein-carbohydrate combination.

- *B Vitamins*

  Getting B vitamins from your diet helps maintain healthy serotonin levels. Vitamins B-1, B-3, B-6 and B-9 (folic acid) all help convert tryptophan into functional serotonin. Eat fortified cereals - they often contain all the B vitamins you need to make serotonin. Fish poultry, seeds, nuts and beans serve as sources of B vitamins, while avocados boost your intake of vitamins B-6 and B-9 and peanuts provide a source of vitamin B-3.

- *Healthy fats, such as omega-3 fatty acids*

  Omega-3 fatty acids are believed to affect the functionality of serotonin in the brain. People with low serotonin levels commonly have low DHA levels, which is an essential building block in the brain, and which needs to be replenished with foods that are high in omega-3 fatty acids such as fish oils (from oily fish such as salmon, mackerel and sardines), chia seeds and flax seeds.

- *Caffeine and Alcohol*

  Limit your caffeine and alcohol consumption as both have been shown to decrease serotonin levels significantly.

Bright Light

Research has found a positive correlation between serotonin synthesis and total hours spent in sunlight during the day. One study showed that the mood-lowering effect of acute tryptophan depletion in healthy women is completely blocked by carrying out the study in bright light instead of dim light. So open your curtains to let light into your home or office and spend time outdoors every day – as often as possible. Exercise outside is great!

Exercise

Exercise causes an increase in tryptophan. The tryptophan persists well after exercising is finished, suggesting that mood elevation and focus can be present for hours after the exercising has finished. Work out at an intensity level that you are familiar with, as consistent serotonin release is linked with exercise that people feel good doing, not exercise that pushes you too hard or that you dislike. Aerobic exercise is ideal but if circumstances make that difficult, walk for 30 minutes a day or dance at home like nobody is watching! Ideally do this in the morning so you set yourself up for a successful day. This might mean walking to work or doing some kind of gym or home exercise.

Visualization

As you now know, on a neurological level your brain does not tell the difference between what is real or imagined. Therefore, reliving happy memories or simply thinking positive images will give your brain a serotonin boost. If you find it difficult to think of happy times (that's not uncommon!), try talking to friends or family and looking at old journals or pictures that trigger positive emotions. Revisit your triumphs and victories and think of compliments you received in the past etc. Really get into it by making it detailed.

Massage

Several studies show that massage therapy helps cut down the stress hormone cortisol while boosting serotonin levels. Not only does a massage relax your body, it allows you to unwind, giving you a perfect opportunity to visualize yourself being super confident, happy and successful! This opens your mind space for clear focus and productivity.

De-Stress

Prolonged periods of stress can deplete serotonin levels. Serious and systematic stress can have an impact on the body's ability to produce and synthesize serotonin. This means that you should stay away from stressful situations as much as possible, and find healthy ways to deal with stress once it comes your way. Yoga, meditation, visualization, relaxation breathing (we will discuss this more in the next chapter), art or dance may help you unwind. Keeping your life balanced will certainly help so make sure to complete the wheel of needs exercise in Chapter 2 and repeat it regularly to monitor your progress. It is important to prioritise your life. The happier and more functional you are, the better position you are in to enjoy life with those around you. Make life balance a must!

CHAPTER 5

Taking Back Your Power

When I started to implement the information I am sharing with you in this book, not only did I start to feel more confident, my overall results in life and business improved dramatically. By "changing my mind" my life and my results became important. I was focused on being the best me, and after a while of experiencing what it is to feel happy, I was determined to feel that way for the rest of my life. However, I must be honest with you, at the beginning I couldn't help but fear that my new way of thinking and my new behaviours wouldn't last, that one day something or someone would take my feeling of confidence and happiness away from me. I feared I might get knocked back in some way and that I would become the old me again, the "failure-Donna-with-no-confidence-that-feared-everything-and-everyone". Those scary "what-ifs" frequently crept into my thoughts; What if someone said something and I didn't know how to react? What if I got hurt again? What if someone didn't like me? What if I was in a situation of confrontation or conflict? What if people judged me or laughed at me? What if I fail? What if I succeed and can't handle it? I worried that I would buckle under the pressures of life.

Fear

It's important to understand that fear is a normal feeling and not something to be ashamed about. We all get afraid and nervous, even the most seemingly high-powered individuals. It's what you do with the feeling that matters, not the feeling itself. Instead of thinking of it as a scary monster that will devour you, I would like you to acknowledge the feeling of fear for what it is, so that if you experience it, you will know exactly what to do. Remember fear is not a thing; it is an emotion that you can regulate back to a feeling of calmness and focus. You are in control of what happens.

Fear, like any emotion, is a chemical and hormonal reaction to a situation we are experiencing, in reality or in our minds. In psychological terminology the reaction we experience is called the *fight or flight response* and it occurs because our brain *perceives* a harmful event or threat. Do we fight the threat or do we flee? You could liken it to an alarm bell ringing if a fire outbreak or burglar is a possibility in your home. It could be a false alarm but it activates on *perceived threat,* not just on actual threat.

When we feel afraid (even nervous) chemicals are released in our body, mostly nor-epinephrine and epinephrine. It is nature's way of priming us for fighting or fleeing. Thousands of years ago this would have been essential to survival. For example, if a tiger came at us we would have needed our brains to react quickly, to let us know if we should stay and fight or run. The system itself is fabulous as its purpose is to keep us from harm. However, sometimes it can over react. No matter how slight or extreme a situation is, real or imagined, if our brain perceives a threat of any kind it will release fear related chemicals, which in turn release cortisol and adrenaline, the major stress hormones. So it is our perception of the threat that determines how much chemicals are released and for how long the stress hormones remain. Cortisol and adrenaline are responsible for the symptoms we get when we panic, such as racing heart, rapid or shallow breathing, shaking, paling or flushing, freezing on the spot, digestion and bladder issues, tunnel vision, pupil dilation, dizziness and erection problems (if you are male). The good thing is that when we know what is happening in our bodies, we can feel more capable of dealing with what is happening. This is where *oxygen-carbon dioxide regulation* comes in. Let me explain why this is important and how it works.

Oxygen – Carbon Dioxide Regulation

When we get a fright or feel nervous our brain sounds the alarm so to speak and activates the fight or flight response, releasing stress hormones as outlined. However, not only does it release hormones, it disrupts our normal oxygen-carbon dioxide input and output process. Under normal calm circumstances, we breathe in oxygen and it enters our red blood cells, where it is carried freely to our brain and used for normal bodily functions. We then breathe out carbon dioxide to keep our bodies regulating nicely and so we feel at ease – a very straightforward process that our brain likes and we do it without even thinking about it.

However, if we get a fright, or feel nervous, sometimes the normal oxygen-carbon dioxide regulation gets disrupted. The brain might assume that we have not enough oxygen to fuel our 'fight or flight' state, and with our survival in mind, starts to panic. Remember, it is our brains' job to keep us safe. It sounds the alarm "Get in oxygen quick or I will die" and directs us to start to breath rapidly (hyperventilate). The result of this hyperventilation however, is that too much carbon dioxide is blown off by our lungs, causing us to shake and feel dizzy and even more anxious. So the key here is to restore the oxygen-carbon dioxide regulatory mechanism, which will allow our brain to relax again. This is actually quite easy to do, believe it or not, a classic example that having knowledge is powerful! To regulate the oxygen-carbon dioxide flow simply do the following exercise. It will bring your body back to a state of equilibrium so you feel calm and relaxed in any situation. It works every time – no exception.

Taking Control: 7-11 Breathing

- Sit comfortably on a chair in an upright position. Once you have practiced this exercise many times, you will find you can do it even standing up.
- Place both hands on your tummy area
- Imagine your tummy to be a balloon that can inflate or deflate. Take a slow breath in through your nose for a count of 7 and breathe out through your mouth for a count of 11. The *shorter in-breathe* and *longer out-breathe* will begin to regulate the oxygen-carbon dioxide flow so it becomes normal again.
- Repeat this 7-11 breathing five times or until you totally relax.
- Once you have done this exercise a few times and you are happy that you've got it, you can do it anywhere. Obviously if you are in public it's probably best you don't place your hand on your tummy. Simply breathe.

Remember, if you feel anxious at any time it is simply a matter of oxygen-carbon dioxide de-regulation. You are in control of what happens next. Acknowledge that your brain is experiencing a *temporary* state of feeling threatened in reaction to something that is happening in your environment, whether that be in reality or in your thoughts, sounds and images in your head. Do not get caught up in the why, just acknowledge the feeling being experienced. It may be a case of a **F**alse **E**xpectation **A**ppearing **R**eal. Start to regulate your breathing by breathing in for a count of 7 and out for a count of 11. As you breathe out say the following affirmation to yourself *"I am okay and I am safe. I can do what I need to do with ease and with confidence. I allow myself to relax."*, whilst imaging yourself carrying out the scenario with confidence.

Note that sometimes, in a calm state it's useful to ask yourself if there is something you need to learn from the situation so that you can be happy in your ability to cope well in the future, no matter what the situation. For example, if you are afraid of delivering a presentation to a group of people is it that you are afraid of messing up and being laughed at (i.e. arising from an old program) or is it a case that you genuinely didn't prepare your presentation properly?

Help your mind and body as much as possible so they will work for your greater good.

The Self-fulfilling Prophecy

Fear is often related to what we believe, i.e. what we fear has happened, is happening or will happen. What do you *believe* about yourself and your life? Do you believe you are capable or incapable, intelligent or stupid, worthy or unworthy, successful or unsuccessful? Your beliefs about yourself are more important than you realise.

In an extensive study by psychologist Albert Bandura it was found that our belief in our capability to manage situations determines how we think, behave, and feel and it directly impacts our results and performance. Robert Rosenthal and Lenore Jacobson showed the power of a self-fulfilling prophecy in a school setting. The study took place in a public elementary school in a predominantly lower-class community. At the beginning of the school year, the researchers gave the students an IQ test called "The Harvard Test of Inflected Acquisition." The teachers at the school were told that this test would determine student IQs, and more importantly could identify students who would make fast, above average academic progress in the coming year, whether or not they were currently "good" students.

Before the next school year began, teachers received the names of those students who, on the basis of their test results, could be *expected* to perform well. They were "academic spurters". In reality, Rosenthal and Jacobson had just randomly picked these names from the class list. The test did not identify academic spurters. The teachers were only led to *believe* that it did. In other words, any differences between the children existed only in the minds of the teachers.

A second IQ test was given at the end of the school year. The students who had been recognised as academic spurters showed an average increase of 12 points on their IQ scores, compared to an increase of 8 points amongst the rest of the students. The differences were even bigger in younger students, with almost half of first and second-grade academic spurters showing an IQ increase of 20 points or more.

Teachers' subjective assessments showed similar differences. They reported that these "special" students were more intellectually curious, better behaved, had greater chances for future success, and were friendlier than the other students.

This tells us that a self-fulfilling prophecy was taking place, i.e. the teachers had encouraged the performance they *expected* to see. They spent more time with the "intelligent" students and they were more eager to teach them. The result was that the "intelligent" students felt more capable and their performance reflected that.

Another example of this at work is the "four-minute mile". Basically runners were consistently achieving times of 4:03, 4:02 and 4:01, but no one could get under four minutes. This led to a common perception that running a mile in less than four minutes was physically impossible. In 1954 Roger Bannister changed that belief with a running time of 3:59. Remarkably, within 18 months of Bannister's breakthrough 16 other athletes ran under 4 minutes. Bannister showed the possibility of breaking the existing threshold so athletes were no longer limited by their old beliefs.

The question is: are the things that you are afraid of, the things that you are allowing to hold you back from being who you are capable of being, are they actual truths or limiting beliefs? Beliefs can be changed if you want or allow them to be and if you open your mind to new possibilities. We used to believe the world was flat and that we'd fall off the edge if we went far enough. Aren't we lucky we changed that belief?!

Sometimes it's just a matter of trusting yourself and your capabilities, even if you don't have self-belief. Expect good things to happen and put the things in place that will help you do that. Give yourself the permission to do something new, visualise an excellent outcome, affirm yourself and then practice, practice, practice until you get the excellent outcome for real. Believe and achieve.

What great things would you do *if you did* believe in yourself? Write them down now.

outcome, affirm yourself and then practice, practice, practice until you get the excellent outcome for real. Believe and achieve.

What great things would you do *if you did* believe in yourself? Write them down now.

____

____

____

____

____

____

____

____

____

____

____

Now ask yourself this: what's actually stopping you from achieving those things now? If you come up with an excuse for not doing those things think of it this way: if I was to give you $1,000,000 or something you really want if you did what you ultimately want to do (without having to wait for "self-belief"), could and would you do it? Of course you could!

Cognitive Dissonance

I'm sure you've heard of the game of tug-a-war, a contest in which two teams pull against each other at opposite ends of a rope with the object of pulling the middle of the rope over a mark on the ground. It's quite a fun game. However, one type of tug-a-war is not fun, the tug-a-war in your mind. You know what I mean, the feeling of discomfort you get when you're torn between two or more contradictory beliefs or behaviours. For example, I used to struggle with eating healthily. It was a daily will I eat or won't I eat struggle. We all have some kind of internal tug-a-war and it's known as *cognitive dissonance*.

When we have beliefs and behaviours that contradict each other we will always experience conflict unless we align our beliefs and behaviours. This is similar to aligning our values with our behaviour. For example, I used to fear being judged by people. How eager do you think I was to accept public speaking opportunities? Not very! Even if I wanted to speak to an audience, I felt I couldn't. My beliefs got in the way.

My internal tug-a-war was as follows:

- I don't want people to judge or laugh at me.
- I have an opportunity to speak in public.
- Public speaking is a situation where people could judge me.
- Conclusion: Decline speaking invitation and

feel upset with myself because *"I didn't have the confidence to do it."*

In order for me to feel okay about accepting invitations to speak in public, I had to replace my old limiting belief with a new productive belief, which turned out to be this:

"I have valuable information and I have an opportunity to share it with people who need it to improve their lives. If I don't deliver my information to them I am denying them an opportunity to enhance their lives".

My love for helping people was stronger than any fear of judgement and with that belief at the fore, how eager did I become about speaking to audiences? Very! Becoming aware of how conflicting beliefs impact the decision-making process is a great way to improve your ability to make better choices.

Once I changed my old belief it was just a matter of improving my speaking skills and practising until I got good at it, which made the delivery better.

There are three key strategies to reduce cognitive dissonance:

- **Focus on a more supportive belief that outweighs the dissonant belief or behaviour.** This is what I did in the public speaking example above. However, it is important that the more supportive belief has strong emotion attached to it so the new behavior is maintained. Emotion is what ultimately drives us. I visualized the results of all the people I helped. It motivated me to help more people.

- **Reduce the importance of the conflicting belief.** For example someone might believe that to be accepted they must look a certain way. This might result in spending endless amounts of time in front of the mirror or buying the best of everything (even if it costs a fortune). However, if they were to stop, review, and realize that life is time limited, perhaps by meeting someone with terminal illness, for example, the perspectives and beliefs might change.
- **Change the conflicting belief so that it is consistent with other beliefs or behaviour.** For example, if you are someone who attaches a negative association to money, believing that wealthy people are greedy or selfish, perhaps you could believe that money can be used as a valuable means to contribute to and help those less fortunate, enabling you to travel to give assistance to those who need it or start a project for those in need. Therefore being wealthy can be a good thing.

Right now, think of a belief that you need to change if you are to get the results you want. Write it opposite.

Based on the information you've read above, how do you need to reframe that belief so your new belief is more productive?

CHAPTER 6

When People Make You Panic

Meeting New People

Meeting and talking to new people, especially in groups or formal situations, is one of the main issues people have when it comes to confidence and success. Indeed it used to be one of my concerns. I worried about what I would say. I worried about what people might say to me. I worried about running out of things to talk about, sounding like an idiot. I used to visualise people thinking I was a loser, not worthy of a conversation, and turning their backs on me.

With time however, I came to the realisation that if I was to become the confident successful person I wanted to become, I would have to change the existing belief I held about myself and move into a more productive way of thinking. Not only that, I had to change my beliefs surrounding situations with people. For example, one belief I had was that if I met someone new, they wouldn't like me. In order for me to allow people into my life I had to reframe that old belief. So instead of focusing on myself, I made the situation about the other person. I thought about the fact that although a person may seem confident, they might *not* be confident. They might be just as nervous as me and talking to them openly was an opportunity for me to *help them* feel good about themselves. My love for helping people to feel good about themselves essentially allowed me to think of meeting people as an opportunity to create something positive, whether that be by including them in a conversation, giving a compliment, placing value on what they had to say etc. With this new belief I felt it was my duty to meet with and talk to people!

How could you look at meeting people differently? What beliefs do you need to have about people to ensure you become confident to succeed? Below write some reframes for your limiting beliefs. Make your focus positive and about the person or situation, not about you. How else could you view a situation?

___

___

___

___

___

___

___

Introducing Yourself

Firstly, remember that you are good enough. You are worthy of any conversation and *nobody* is superior to you. Any person you meet is a regular person with worries and sufferings of their own. Indeed they may be feeling as fearful as you are. No matter what they look like, what they have, who they know, what they say or how successful or perfect they seem to be, underneath it all we are just regular imperfect human beings. To make conversation instantly easy for you I have outlined some great techniques below for you to use and practice. These techniques are those that I used and practiced to become confident.

1) **Understand that the person you are talking to is not perfect**

   Think about it, every person you talk to has cried at some point (many times!) and therefore they are just as vulnerable as you were. Everyone has messed up, everyone has "failed" and everyone has moments of sadness. We all wake up looking dishevelled and we all go to sleep tired. Even the most confident people snore! People are people, see them as such.

2) **Make eye contact**

   It shows that you're interested in talking to the person, as well as displaying confidence. Looking away makes it look as though you're bored. If you're not comfortable looking straight into someone's eyes, look at the point between their eyebrows now and then – they won't notice the difference.

Keep it natural – the average person doesn't look at someone for more than three seconds at a time anyway. As you get used to meeting people eye contact will come natural to you.

3) **Smile**

Smiling portrays a positive attitude and people like to be around positive people. There's no need to go overboard, just think of what it is to be in a happy upbeat state. Put yourself in a positive posture and it's easy to do this.

4) **Say "Hello"!**

It's the simplest but most effective ice-breaker. Speak in a positive, upbeat tone of voice that shows that you're happy with what you do. Again, maintain a positive upbeat posture and it will come naturally to you.

5) **Offer a handshake**

When you shake someone's hand give them a firm handshake. You don't need to squeeze their hand off, just make it firm enough to show them that you are confident. There is nothing worse than someone shaking your hand and it being limp and if your hands tend to get sweaty, wipe them before you offer a handshake!

6) **Make a relevant comment**

Initiate a conversation by making a relevant

comment about something that is happening at the time. For example, if you find yourself at a charity event, you might like to ask the person how they got involved in the charity or what brought them to the event. Speak as though you would to a trusted family member.

7) **Ask Open-ended Questions**

   In order to keep a conversation going it's best to use open-ended questions. Open-ended questions are those that start with the words *How, Why, Where* or *What*. They allow for elaboration. Usually when somebody feels fearful of meeting people they unintentionally engage in closed questions, i.e. questions that allow for a yes or no answer only, with very little room for elaboration. For example, if I ask someone "Have you been to this event before?" the answer could be a simple yes or no and that could be the end of the conversation. However, if I was to ask "*How* did you get involved in the charity?" the person has to elaborate, which opens up room for further conversation.

8) **Validate**

   Once the line of communication has been opened up, the next thing is to create solid rapport. This means getting the person on side so they want to talk more. The easiest way to do this is to focus on the person you are talking to (not you) and validate them, listen to them, hear what they are saying and help them feel important and valued. Everyone loves to feel important and valued! This does not mean being false or pretending you like them, it is merely allowing them to feel valued as a human being, which you should do anyway. It may surprise you that many people feel devalued. If you give someone a sense of genuine positive importance you will be noted – guaranteed. After all, who doesn't like feeling validated and valued? You can do this easily by first listening to what they say (we all love being listened to) and comment using phrases that are relevant to what was said. For example you may say "That's very interesting", "That's a great point/ question." or "That was a great thing to do." Make it solid.

9) **Repeat the name of the person you meet**

Repeating the name of a person you meet does two things:

- It allows the person you are talking to feel important and shows that you're really listening and care about what he or she has to say.
- It helps you remember their name for future reference. It is amazing how easily we forget people's names after a conversation yet it is so important to pay attention to remember it.

Example: "Hi, Rita" (at the beginning of the conversation)..."That's interesting, Rita." (during the conversation)... "It was great to chat with you, Rita," or "It was nice to meet you, Rita," (at the end of the conversation).

10) **Focus on the positive**

An introductory conversation is no time to tell your woe-is-me stories. People don't want to know about your struggles when they first meet you. It gives the impression that you could be hard work to be around. Allow people to feel good when they are in your company. They will like you more for it and will want to be around you.

Confrontation

Just mentioning the word confrontation is enough to make a lot of people break out in a sweat. This is, in part, due to a belief that when you challenge someone it will be met with defense, the relationship will end up worse off than it was before, or that the person being confronted won't like you anymore. This does not have to be the case at all. Many people are brought up with the notion that confrontation always has to get ugly, with aggression and defensive behaviour being inevitable. Although confrontation can get ugly, it doesn't have to. When you understand confrontation and handle it correctly, it actually strengthens the relationship by opening up lines of communication and removing obstacles to a deeper connection.

Understanding Confrontation

Scenario: Mary wanted to confront her husband about

the fact that he never picked up his dirty laundry off the floor. Every day, he left the dirty clothes on the floor, for someone else to place into the washing machine. Realizing that this was a small thing, she just put the clothes into the washer herself. But it still bothered her and every day, when she saw those dirty clothes on the ground, she got just a little more irritated until, finally one day she had enough, and she couldn't take it anymore. She took the dirty clothes, stomped over to where her husband was sitting on the sofa and fired the clothes at him, screaming that she was not his mother and it was not her job to clean up after his "disrespectful ass". His reaction was less than accommodating and so the screaming match began.

The reason it got ugly: Mary let the problem fester until she exploded. Every time she saw the dirty clothes on the floor she believed it was yet another sign of disrespect. It was as if he was offending her over and over again.

The main problem with confrontation is that what we actually want to confront is often not reflected in what we say. When we get clear on what our own motivations are, on what we're really trying to accomplish and allow ourselves to deal with others in a productive way, we allow for much better relationships. Conversations become less about assigning blame, and more about understanding, responsibility and compromise, both in professional and personal settings. It means you will be confident to speak your mind and ask for what you want in a way that others will happily consider. You'll begin to see others in a new light – not as rivals that you need to protect yourself from, but as other creators that you get to play with.

Prepare

- Figure out what belief is being triggered and question if it's accurate and useful. For example an employer may believe that his employee is careless and lazy because she delivers poor reports, when in fact the employee may not have an efficient system to do the reports.
- Determine what it is that you *really* want the outcome to be. Do you just want the person to admit that they are wrong or do you want to clear the air so they do something different to what they have been doing? Focus on the end goal, the outcome you truly want. Make sure that the outcome you're focusing on is a win-win. If you're secretly just trying to be "right", instead of actually trying to resolve a conflict, things are not going to turn out well.
- Focus on what you DO want, not on what you DON'T want. For example, instead of thinking, "I want her to stop ignoring the instructions I give her", focus on "I want her to deliver her work on time and in the format I requested."
- Make sure you're not making any assumptions that

you have no proof of. The person is unlikely to be doing this to you on purpose. They probably have no idea that their behavior is upsetting you. So take the approach that this is a misunderstanding and work from there.

- Expect a positive outcome. Play out a successful scenario in your mind like a movie.

Confront with Confidence

- *Maintain a productive attitude and stay calm*
  You're not defending yourself against an attack, so don't expect one. You're simply providing information to another person. Remember, assume that they did not mean to upset you and they may have no idea how you feel.
- *Time it right*
  Starting a confrontation while in the heat of the moment may be one of the things that got you in trouble in the past. This is because when upset or angry, we don't think in the most articulate way. If you feel anger start to boil inside of you, take a minute and walk away. There is no shame in telling the other person that you'll get back to them as soon as possible in order to gather yourself and think in a more constructive way, i.e. when you're emotional brain isn't on overdrive. Take at least 15 minutes out and come back. Your logical brain will be back in the driver seat after that time.

- *Use "I"*
  Never start a confrontation with "You...". It has a connotation of blame attached to it, implying there is some accusatory emotion or motive behind their behavior, which will immediately cause the person to be on guard and defensive. Instead, use the word "I...". For example, instead of saying "You obviously don't care" you could say "When you do that, *I feel* upset by it." These two statements are going to elicit very different responses. Own your feelings, not theirs.
- *Get the real story*
  The person may have a perfectly valid reason for doing what they're doing. So, before you ask them to make a change, find out why they're doing it their way in the first place. Ask questions, maintaining a tone of curiosity not of accusation.
- *Start doing*
  Don't ask the other person to stop something, but rather to start doing something different. For example, instead of an employer asking an employee to stop delivering poor reports, he could request that she start doing them another way instead. Approach it with a positive statement, such as "I know you've been working hard lately and I appreciate your efforts." From there, make the statement you need to make and then give the other person a chance to respond. Don't retaliate

or make unsubstantiated claims or say anything derogatory. Stick to the facts, make your point or request, and ask that the other person take some time to think about it. This allows you to stay in control of the confrontation so you are more confident with it.

Public Speaking

By the time we are just ten years of age most of us have felt anxious at the thought of speaking in front of a group. This should come as no surprise considering we are conditioned at school to feel bad if we do not perform well in front of our peers. I remember when I was a kid sitting next to a boy who dreaded public speaking, in that he would sometimes nearly cry when asked to read aloud to the class. He found it difficult to read to himself never mind to a group of children that were inevitably going to laugh at him. What's worse is that the teacher subtly encouraged people to laugh as he stumbled from one word to the next, using him as some kind of tool to make sure the rest of us practiced our reading. Truth be told, watching that poor boy cringe in terror must have rubbed off on me. I too was terrified to read aloud, not because I couldn't read (I was very good at reading) but because I feared stumbling up. I believed that I would be judged and laughed at. In a desperate effort to save myself from ridicule I would skip ahead, predicting where I might have to read from after the person next to me had read their bit. My heart would pound in my chest, like a Gorilla banging a drum. Truth be told, I think I would have preferred to eat dirty socks! I felt utterly choked by "fear". Public speaking just wasn't for me. However, now I speak on stage to thousands of people and I speak on TV and radio without even an ounce of fear. How so? How did I go from fearing public speaking so much to absolutely loving it? I will show you here.

Change Perception!

If you fear public speaking an old program from a previous experience is still active. You may or may not know what that program is and it's not essential that you do. You just need to scramble how you currently "perceive" public speaking if it's not useful. In a moment you will learn how to scramble programmes.

Scrambling Programmes

Think for a moment about what you believe will happen if you speak in public. What scenario do you see playing out in your mind? How do you look? What do others look like? Where are you? What do you hear? Are people talking? What are they saying? Do you hear shuffling? etc. Write it down here if it makes it easier to imagine.

____

____

____

____

____

____

____

____

Now I want you to *intentionally* scramble that imagined scenario by doing the following:

Step1

- Instead of seeing the scenario in colour, I want you to turn it into a black and white version. Imagine watching a recording of yourself in that situation. See it play on the TV in black and white mode.
- Imagine the *volume being turned down and then off* as though you are muting the TV. So if you hear people talking mute them so their mouths move but no words come out.
- imagine the TV shrinking so small that it fits in your hands.
- Imagine squashing the TV to bits and then imagine throwing it away.

Step 2

- Bring up an image in your mind of you speaking to a group or on stage really successfully. See yourself confident and at ease. Your delivery is perfect and people are responding really well to you. See them interested in what you have to say. If you are giving a speech, imagine people eagerly taking notes. See them clapping at the end of your speech and feel the pride of knowing you did a great job. If you are speaking to a new person or a group of people, see yourself confident and self assured. Amp it up. Make it bright, beautiful and successful!
- Remember, the psycho-cybernetic loop? Use it here. As you visualise your positive outcome, maintain a strong confident posture right the way through. Look up, pull your shoulders back and allow yourself to feel upbeat. If you don't have to stand behind a podium, walk around to show the audience how comfortable you are.
- Rehearse this new successful scenario in your mind over and over. This new positive perception will soon become the reality for your brain. Trust me, do it and you'll see!

The Reality of Public Speaking

Remind yourself that each person in the audience is just a regular individual, not a blob of judgemental scariness. They each have regular lives and they are all just regular people who happen to be in the same place at the same time. Nobody is superior. We all get up in the morning looking scruffy and we all lounge on our couches in the evening, no matter what we portray to others. Feel what it is to be in the room with regular people and instead of seeing them as judgmental, speak to them as friends. The following tips will make this easier for you.

- *Select three people in the audience*
  Two from the front row (one on the far right and the other on the far left) and one person at the back of the room in the centre. Think of these three people as regular friends and speak to them, even if there are ten thousand people in the room. Because you're looking left, right and then centre back everyone in the audience thinks you are talking to them. It works every time!
- *Know what you're talking about*
  Although it's possible to bluff your way through a talk, it's very important that you don't! Firstly, people don't like listening to regurgitated scripts so you'll very easily lose your audience if you present script style. Secondly, if someone asks you a question during your talk or side tracks you you'll be in trouble as you won't know how to get back on track. Instead, know what you're talking about! It will allow you to feel relaxed and happy in the knowledge that no matter what happens or what

anyone says or asks you will always be able to handle it with an air of confidence and composure.

The easiest way to learn and remember material is to discuss the topics with a few people well in advance of your speech. Let them ask you questions, contradict you on purpose, ask you to elaborate etc. It gives you time to research anything you stumbled on in your discussions.

- *Speak to your audience*

  Keep in mind that you are merely sharing information with your audience you are not there to talk *at* them. People hate it when they don't understand what a presenter is saying so leave the fancy words aside. Instead speak in easy-to-understand language, as though talking to a friend, and inject passion into what you are saying. Get excited about sharing what you know and people will pick up on it.

CHAPTER 7

Failure and Success

What do these people have in common - Walt Disney, Thomas Edison, Bill Gates, Henry Ford, Albert Einstein, VincentVan Gough, Steven Spielberg, Richard Branson and Michael Jordan? Would it surprise you if I told you that they were all documented failures? Yes, failures! All of these people, people we now recognise as great achievers, geniuses even, were all categorised as failures at one point in their lives. They were laughed at, considered crazy and stupid, and their work and abilities were belittled. They were reminded often, and no doubt believed, that they were not successful. Can you imagine how unconfident they might have felt?

Walt Disney. He was fired by a newspaper editor because, "he lacked imagination."

Thomas Edison: Teachers told Edison he was "too stupid to learn anything." He was fired from his first two jobs for not being productive enough. And he made over 1,000 unsuccessful attempts at inventing the light bulb before its success.

Bill Gates: He dropped out of Harvard and started a

business that "failed". It was only later that he created, Microsoft, one of the most successful companies in the world.

Henry Ford: His early businesses failed. He was broke five times before he founded the hugely successful Ford Motor Company.

Albert Einstein: He didn't speak until he was four years old and he didn't read until he was seven. His teachers and parents thought he was "handicapped" and anti-social. He was expelled from school. Now schools teach his wisdom.

Vincent Van Gogh: During his lifetime, Van Gogh sold only one painting. Today, any of the 800+ paintings he painted during his life are worth a fortune.

Steven Spielberg: He was rejected from the University of Southern California School of Theater, Film and Television three times. He attended college at another location but dropped out to become a director. In 2002, thirty-five years after starting his degree, he returned to complete his studies and earn his BA.

Richard Branson: He dropped out of high school. Today, he is considered one of the most successful men in the world.

Michael Jordan: He was cut from his high school basketball team. He "missed more than 9,000 shots, lost almost 300 games and on 26 occasions missed the winning shot he was entrusted to make." Now he is known to many as the best basketball player of all time.

Failure

By definition failure is "a state of inability to perform a normal function or an omission of occurrence or performance. It is a defect in character, conduct, or ability". In simple terms failure translates as disaster. Considering the achievements of all fore mentioned, I think it is fair to say that the term has been so often misused and misplaced. The truth of the matter is whether someone becomes a "failure" is determined by what they choose to accept and believe. A problem only occurs when we internalise how it feels when we don't achieve the goal we set out to achieve or when someone tries to belittle our efforts. If we nominalise the experience and "failure" becomes our identity to the point where not achieving a goal is somehow proof that we are inadequate, this is a sure way to affect how confident we feel! Most of us will stumble and fall in life. Doors will get slammed in our faces, and we might make some bad decisions but that does not mean we are failures. A "failure" is just a made up concept by people who don't have a broad enough perspective to see beyond current results. Failure is not a constant, it is not a thing or person, and it certainly isn't you!

Imagine if Michael Jordan, having missed shot after shot during his basketball career, decided that because he didn't get the result he and his team wanted he was a failure. He probably would have given up on his dream of becoming a world class player. And imagine if Thomas Edison gave up on the light bulb. I might have had to write this book (and you read it) under candle light!

The Fear of Being Inadequate

Feeling adequate or inadequate is such a big part of most people's psyche and it can affect how confident we feel as a whole. We like to feel liked and approved of. We set standards for ourselves and standards are set by others for us, right from the moment we are born. We are conditioned to feel proud when we achieve and to feel bad when we don't. At school we get gold stars when we do well in exams and we are made fun of when we don't. At work we get promotions and pay rises when we perform and get shunned upon when we don't. We are conditioned to enjoy approval and dislike rejection, and depending on how deep the feelings attached to approval and rejection are, will determine the reaction we have to a goal being achieved or not achieved. If not achieving a goal means emotional pain for us, we will avoid "failing" wherever and whenever we can, especially when it involves possible judgement from other people. Remember, our brain's aim is to keep us feeling comfortable and safe.

To illustrate how impactful the fear of failure can be I will tell you about a friend of mine. For the purposes of this book, let's call him Paul. For years Paul was admired by his community and family. His high powered job allowed him to have a lavish lifestyle – the big house, the flashy car, the best of clothes etc. He was known for his high standards and affluence. Little did he know that due to economical difficulties he would lose his company and all the money that resulted from it. Feeling like an absolute failure Paul couldn't bring himself to tell his family. He was ashamed and didn't know how to handle what might mean change and a very different lifestyle for all involved. So instead of telling them, he got up every morning "for work" as usual and returned home at the usual time, leading them to think that everything was normal. He would even take his briefcase. This went on for six weeks until he finally broke down and came clean. He dreaded being rejected by those who had held him in such high regard. He dreaded his family thinking he was a failure. The idea of not being the high powered man frightened him so much that he felt he had to hide it.

However, Paul actually had no solid evidence that people would think any less of him. In fact, it turned out that his family and friends were more than supportive. Paul's feelings were not based on any evidence they were based on his perception of the situation. And perceptions can, more often than not, be way off the mark.

FEAR = **F**alse **E**xpectation **A**ppearing **R**eal.

As soon as Paul opened up to his family and friends he was surprised to hear that they had already noticed that he wasn't himself. They knew something was wrong but they just didn't know how to approach the subject or how to help. You see you can pretend everything is rosy but people prefer it when you're real. Any situation can be worked on but only when you are honest and open about it. That does not mean you have to tell the world how you feel, it's just important that you are open with those who matter.

Feedback versus Failure

Everyone experiences setbacks in one way or another but it is how you view a setback that determines how quickly you will bounce back from it. You ultimately have two choices: 1) view the set back as *failure,* get weighed down by it, and give up or 2) view the setback as *feedback,* i.e. an opportunity to learn something from the experience (this may mean asking for help) so you can formulate or refine a strategy for better results. Pick yourself up, dust yourself off and start again.

Imagine starting out on a car journey to a certain destination, to somewhere you've never been before. Having looked at your map and chosen your route, you begin driving. Everything is great, the scenery is beautiful and your excitement starts to build as you get closer to your destination. You are on track and you feel confident in your ability to get there. Then suddenly your oil light comes on. You panic, realising that you didn't bring a spare oil can and the next gas station is miles away. You have no choice but to stop the car and wait for someone to come and help.

Unfortunately you are on a quiet country road with very little traffic (you chose the scenic route!) so you know that you might have to wait a while. You can't call anyone as it would mean them travelling for miles to rescue you, and you don't want to ask them for help anyway, in case they get annoyed or think you are stupid for not checking your oil in the first place. Sitting in your car you feel alone, helpless and frustrated, analysing how you let yourself get into this situation in the first place: *'How could I be so stupid?'*, *'Why did I not check my oil before I left?'*, *'Why did I not bring spare oil?'*

An hour passes and still nobody arrives.

Then all of a sudden you notice in your mirror a car approaching. With a huge feeling of relief, you quickly jump out of the car and wave for assistance. To your horror, instead of stopping to help you, the driver of the car just flies passed you as though you didn't exist. Your heart sinks. It's beginning to get dark and, feeling very alone you realise you may have to sleep in your car for the night. You feel utterly hopeless and have no idea what to do.

Your only solution is to call someone and ask them to come and get you, the last thing you want to have to do. Assuming that the person on the other end of the phone will bark down the phone at you, you cringe as you dial in the number. But to your absolute amazement they have no issue whatsoever driving to you to help you. In fact they are more than delighted to help you.

So your options are to either view the experience as *failure or feedback*. If you choose to believe you failed you will not only feel bad, you will prevent yourself from learning and creating new opportunities. If you view the experience as feedback however you can learn how to get better results the next time and create better opportunities.

For example, from the above example, you could either give yourself a hard time about making a mistake or you might learn to:

1) Prepare better. Check your car thoroughly before you go on a long drive.
2) Take a straightforward route if you are driving alone.
3) Realise that it's okay to ask for help and ask for it as soon as you feel you need it. You do not have to wait for people to know you need help.

Moving Forward

Worrying about failure keeps you focused on the past and the problems. If you are to feel confident in your ability to be, do or have anything you must shift your focus onto possibilities and move forward. In addition to this it is important to know whether you are on the right path towards attaining your outcome. Feedback allows you do just that – gather more information so that you stay on track and learn how to overcome any unexpected obstacles along the way. With feedback, you get to know how much progress you have made thus far.

"The definition of insanity is doing the same thing over and over and expecting a different result."
– Albert Einstein

Look for feedback in an experience so you can change or refine your strategy for better results. To make this easier you could ask yourself the following questions:

- What am I aiming to achieve?

- What feedback have I had so far (good and bad)?

- What lessons have I learned?

- How can I put the lessons to positive use?

- How can I improve my strategy?

- How will I measure my success going forward?

- What do I need to do to *now* to pick myself up and have another go?

When Success Can Be a Problem

The definition of success varies from person to person. There is no standard formula. However, we all recognise success as something we strive to attain. It would be fair to assume then that success is something we would all get excited about attaining. If only it was that simple. Statistically success is feared more than failure!

Many people are conditioned to believe that success is something bad. Having been nominalised by society, it is seen as a *thing* we can attain, get or have, which gives it automatic power to define us. For example, some religious orders frown on success, portraying it as something evil that takes over spirituality. When I was a child I was told by a priest that successful people are evil greedy people and that I should avoid success in order to maintain my integral spirit. This belief was supported by many people in my culture so needless to say I received a pretty strong negative program about success. As a result do you think I might have had an issue with becoming successful? I dreaded the very idea of it. I was afraid to be, do and have anything that was "above my station", in case it changed me for the worse. Unfortunately, this is the case for so many people, more than you could ever imagine.

Although on the surface success can seem like something good to want and strive for, for some people the possible implications of being successful can outweigh the rewards of success. If being successful implies pain, becoming successful is likely to be sabotaged. This usually, but not always, happens at an unconscious level.

Fearing success is likely to be an issue for you if:

- You don't complete your projects (at home or in work)
- You talk about what you are going to do more than what you actually do.
- You work furiously on several projects at once, not really focusing deeply on any one of them.
- You still have the same projects that were there five years ago.
- You second-guess yourself often.
- You get easily distracted,
- You worry if your work is good enough.
- And the big giveaway... you're on the verge of success and everything starts to fall apart.

Implications of Success

- *Being unspiritual*

  As a society our relationship with success, money and spirituality has always been a complicated one, tightly woven with our personal integrity. It's like success and money symbolize what we want and don't want, what we get and can't get, what we'd give away and hold on to, what we'd die for and live for. Unfortunately, we have grown to believe that successful people are 'selfish, greedy, shallow, materialistic, and up-themselves' - making your own success a struggle. If I am to become successful will people think bad things about me? Will they think I am selfish, greedy, shallow, materialistic, and up-myself? That's none of their business! Other people's thoughts are not mine to manage.

- *Losing Control*
  As discussed earlier in the book, having a sense of control is essential to a balanced lifestyle. That said it is common for people to fear losing their sense of control as a result of becoming successful. The idea of possibly having to take on a lot of responsibility can be overwhelming. How will I handle the pressure? How will I deal with recognition? How will I influence what people think of me?
- *Meeting Expectations*
  Having to live up to people's expectations can be a daunting prospect. What if I mess up? What if I can't maintain success? How will I be perceived? Playing small can act as a way to avoid expectations.
- *Standing Out*
  The fear of standing out can bring some people to their knees. Getting attention or being in the limelight carries with it the possibility of rejection or indeed making someone else feel inadequate. The truth is not everyone will like you and not

everyone will feel adequate standing next to you, but you are not responsible for them.

- *Change*
  Change is a natural part of life, nothing ever stays the same. However, we can make it so it *feels* the same. Routine and habits allow us to do this easily. Success brings un-charted territory and the "not knowing" can be scary. Imagine if you've been timid for years. What might it be like to be confident? How will you behave? Who will you hang out with? Imagine if you've been a minimum wage employee all your working life and you have an opportunity to become a wealthy business owner. Would you have to get new friends? Will your relationship change? etc. Change can be liberating or it can be terrifying, depending on how you see it, but one thing for sure it that change is inevitable so you might as well steer it in the direction of something you want!
- *Loneliness*
  Many people, particularly women, believe that success makes you more vulnerable to loneliness, that somehow being powerful enough to create the life you want will render you unlovable. It is true that some people will be happy for your success but it is possible that others will feel slighted and envious. Being successful does not make you responsible for other people's sense of self worth.

"Our deepest fear is not that we are
inadequate.
Our deepest fear is that we are powerful
beyond measure.
It is our light, not our darkness that
most frightens us.
We ask ourselves, Who am I to be brilliant, gorgeous,
talented, fabulous?
Actually, who are you not to be?
You are a child of God.
Your playing small does not serve the world.
There is nothing enlightened about shrinking
so that other people won't feel insecure
around you.
We are all meant to shine, as children do.
We were born to make manifest the glory of
God that is within us.
It's not just in some of us; it's in everyone.
And as we let our own light shine,
we unconsciously
give other people permission
to do the same.
As we are liberated from our own fear, our
presence automatically liberates others."

– Marianne Williamson

What Success Really Means

I would like to invite you at this point to begin seeing the concept of success in a new way. Instead of thinking it as a *thing* to be frightened of, see it for what it actually is: an opportunity to do what you were put here to do and inspire others to do. You were born to reach your potential, not shy away from it in an effort to please other people's perceptions and expectations. Remember, what other people think of you is none of your business. Your only business is your own and that is to **be the best *you* can be**. You do not need to measure up in any way to anybody or anything.

Success is a moment-to-moment experience, never a constant. All you need to do is to focus on now, on *this moment* only. Ask yourself how you can be the best you can be in this moment. When you focus on this moment and making it the best you can make it, the moments to follow will take care of themselves.

Success = *the outcome* of a string of moments in which you are being the best *you* can be.

Knowing the above to be true, how can success possibly be a bad thing? Can you think of anything wrong with being the best you can be? Would you have a problem with someone who was doing their best? I doubt it. And if anyone has a problem with someone being the best they can be how about we just feel sorry for them and do our own thing regardless?

I would like you now to write down ten benefits of

your being *successful*. For example, what great thing would you allow yourself to do that you have been putting off? Who will you help by being successful? How confident will you feel knowing you are successful? Etc.

1) ______________________________

2) ______________________________

3) ______________________________

4) ______________________________

5) ______________________________

6) ______________________________

7) ______________________________

8) ______________________________

9) ______________________________

10)______________________________

You were born to be amazing! Embrace it.

CHAPTER 8

Relationships

Relationships make life interesting and worthwhile. They are the building blocks for a fulfilled life and for a productive business. That said, so many people struggle with relationships (personal and business), even the most confident looking individuals; CEOs, actors, famous singers, models, politicians – they all have relationship struggles at times! After all, at the heart of every relationship is trust and trust is not something we give easily, especially to people we don't know. Judgment is also a big factor. Let's face it, who wants to be judged? But the reality is we can never control how someone will react to us. Meeting someone for the first time, getting to know them or maintaining a relationship are all things that take trust, time and practice. So if you find relationships difficult, don't worry about it. It's very normal – and common!

To help you feel confident and build successful relationships just implement what I show you here and practice it often. For the purposes of this book I will show you how you can establish and or improve both your personal and business relationships. They are equally important and can be equally challenging for most people.

A Successful Personal Relationship

It is human nature to want connection to other people. We actually need it. However, in today's world, establishing a meaningful relationship can prove difficult. First of all, we can hold ourselves to ridiculous standards and secondly many people have gone from socializing in person to socializing online. To illustrate just how many people struggle to establish a relationship, let me ask you this question: How many people a year do you think try online dating? 1,000,000? 10,000,000? 15,000,000? In 2014 the recorded figures for the total number of people in the U.S. alone was 41,250,000! (Source: Reuters, Herald News, PC World, Washington Post) What if we extended that to the rest of the world? - The numbers would become colossal! So, if all these people are online searching for love what does it tell us? Well for a start it tells us that millions of people are looking for *connection*. Secondly it tells us that they may not feel confident in their ability to meet people offline.

The reality is interacting face-to-face with someone can feel scary, especially the initial stages as rejection is a possibility. Many people experience that vulnerable feeling, the feeling where you question how well you will be received. 'Am I good enough?' 'Will they think

I'm boring?' 'What if they don't like me?' 'What if they make fun of me?' 'What if they are already in a relationship?' 'What if I look stupid?', 'I got hurt in a relationship before. This person could do the same.' etc. For this reason online dating can be more appealing than face-to-face interaction; the emotional involvement is minimized and it's easy to create a persona that people will like.

The Truth about People

It's easy to scare ourselves into thinking that we are not good enough or worthy enough to establish a relationship with someone we like. However, I ask that you embrace the reality that we are all just human beings, no one superior to another, so why should you question your self-worth or rate yourself any less than another human being? Even if the person you are attracted to is drop-dead-gorgeous and ticks every box under the umbrella of your ideal partner, they are not perfect. They are human; they have fears and concerns of their own, possibly similar to yours or even more extreme than yours. Besides, it is not your place (and you have no right) to decide what someone else thinks or wants; you must give them the opportunity to decide for themselves. You do *not* know what they are thinking. You only assume you do. And what did assume do? It made an **ass** out of **u** and **me**. For all you know, the person may want to approach you as much as you want to approach them; they may be worried about getting knocked back by you! Did you ever think of that? As with anything in life there is always the possibility of something not working out the way you want or someone not reciprocating your advances but how on earth are you supposed to get a relationship unless you give yourself the opportunity to make it happen? Telling yourself that someone may not like you or they may not want you etc. is setting yourself up for disaster. If you struggle with relationships, don't you think it's long overdue that you stop talking yourself out of what could be an amazing experience! Here's how:

1) *Manage Your State*

   As detailed in Chapter 4, you must adopt and maintain a physiology for confidently approaching and/or interacting with the person you want to talk to. Think of people who are confident in this way. May I emphasise the word confident here, not cocky. We want you to be natural. Think of someone that you may or may not know personally who seems to have the confident state nailed. How do they stand or sit? What is their body language like? What emotions are they portraying? Are they smiling naturally? Do they look interested in the person they are talking to? etc.

2) *Turn Down the Volume*

   I want you to think of a time when you wanted to

approach a person but out of feeling nervous or afraid you didn't. Bring up that time in your mind. See yourself in the situation as it was. What did you say to yourself that made you nervous or afraid? Take a moment to think about it and write it down here.

____

____

____

____

____

____

____

____

Now do the following:

- Look at the volume dial overleaf.
- Imagine the dial as being in your brain. You are in full control of it and you can adjust the volume whatever way you like.
- Choose one of the sentences that you wrote above and imagine saying it to yourself now. Just hear the words in your mind.
- Now take control of the volume of that sentence by turning your dial down three notches. See the

dial moving and as it does hear the sound of your voice getting quieter.

- Turn the dial down another few notches and hear the sentence getting even quieter.
- Turn the volume down all the way until you can't hear it anymore.

3) *Focus On the Outside*

When you are interacting with someone you must focus the majority of your attention on what is happening on the outside only, i.e. you will focus on the person in front of you and the people you are with. Make the person feel noticed. Imagine they are wearing a sign that says 'Help me feel important.'

Help Me Feel Important

Your aim is to allow the person to feel valued in your presence. People in general don't feel valued so by you allowing the person to feel valued, they will associate positive feelings with you. Show them you value them by listening to and showing interest in what they have to say. This will be natural if you like them. If you find them boring or not your type, you'll have saved yourself a bad date. If they seem interesting you will naturally want to be with them. Ask open ended question that allow for elaboration. It gives you an opportunity to learn more about them, which is always a good thing!

4) *Keep Your Mood Upbeat*

Never, ever, ever relay your sob stories when you first meet someone you would like to date. It will kill the conversation and create a negative association with you. You do not want people to meet up with you again just because they feel sorry for you (that is what counsellors are for), your aim should be to create positive feelings *only*! Talk about good things and speak well of others. Never criticise or engage in conversation that is critical of anyone. And importantly never put yourself down. It's not attractive. Instead say a simple 'Thank you' to any compliment you are given.

Handling the Possibility of a "No"

Don't take it personally if someone says no to you. There are all sorts of reasons why someone might say no that has absolutely nothing to do with you. For example, they may already be in a relationship or they may just have come out of one, in which case timing might be wrong. Or maybe they just don't feel a connection with you, which may simply be due to different interests or values (not that they don't like you), in which case you will have avoided what could possibly have been a very boring or fiery relationship. Or it could be that they have a different life direction to yours or that their goals are different. Or they might just be having a bad day and don't want to talk to anyone. The reason for rejection could be anything but one thing I can say for certain is that it's unlikely to be out of malice or to be unkind or that they don't like *you*. Liken it to going into a store and seeing a shirt you like, only to realise it's not in your size. You could try to squeeze into the shirt and as a result be uncomfortable, or you could do the smart thing and go to another store where you might find an equally nice (or nicer!) shirt. No = **N**ext **O**pportunity.

The important thing to remember is that no one in this world can appeal to everyone's tastes and no two people are automatically matched. Each person (including you) has preferences, so if you get a no, it just means that you don't fit the description of what the other person wants. You are good enough regardless of other people's preferences; it's just a matter of continuing to "Try on" until you get one that fits, and you will. When you do find a fit then a matter of deciding if it's something you want to keep long term, i.e. establish a relationship. And if a relationship is something you decide on you must make sure it's not just a good fit, it must be a *value match*.

A Value Match

Most people want a meaningful relationship at some point in their lives, even those who choose to have casual dates first. It is in our nature to want to feel like we belong and that we matter to someone. The problem is however that many people don't know what a good relationship is let alone how to establish one, so they either end up in a relationship that isn't good for them (or good for the other person involved) or they simply don't enter a relationship at all. Some of this in my opinion is due to the fact that society has turned the focus of finding a meaningful relationship with someone we have gotten to know to having casual pre-relationship flings. It's unfortunate considering there is a relatively straightforward way of identifying someone you will hit it off with, someone who you will feel genuinely happy with now and long term, a person who will encourage and support you, a person who will add that extra sparkle to your life, a person who you will naturally smile with. The key to it is simple: Ascertain if and how your values match.

When two people meet for the first time, they do not know very much about what the other person values, i.e. what is most important to them in life. Each one makes superficial assumptions about the other, some of which are true while others are false. Yet, over time, if they discover that they agree on their most important values (moral values especially), their relationship will deepen and grow stronger. If they don't agree it will become destructive or it will end.

In order for two people to have a great connection they do not necessarily have to share the same interests or hobbies but they do have to have similar core values if the relationship is to be a good one. For example if one person values honesty and the other does not problems will arise, if there is a situation in which lying occurs. Or if one person values family and the other does not there will be conflict if one wants to have a family day and the other wants to watch a football game, etc. However, if both people value honesty and both people value family, happy days all round.

So in order for you to feel confident in your ability to establish and maintain a relationship all you need to do is look at a person's values. See it that you are in control of who you *choose* to be with and that you will no longer settle for people out of desperation or feeling lonely.

If the person you are interested in shares the same values as you, by all means invite them into your life to learn more about them. It may turn into something great. However, if it is obvious that someone does not match your values don't pursue them. It is a waste of your time and energy. Get choosey!

Live as a Whole

It is important that you stay in control of your decisions and standards in life, not depend on someone else to find you, be impressed by you or make you feel worthy. Live as a *whole*, not a half. The happiest most confident relationship is one where two *whole* people walk on the path of life together hand-in-hand, not one where one person becomes the other's half. A person who truly values you and is confident enough in themselves will want you to be a happy whole person they can enjoy being with.

A Successful Business Relationship

The success of your business is determined by the quality of your business relationships. If you don't have good business relationships, you won't have a good business. Fortunately, and maybe to your surprise, it is actually quite easy to create good business relationships if you understand how they work. And you'll be delighted to know that in this book you will learn exactly how to do it!

However, before we do this, it's important that you understand a business relationship is just another interaction with a human being – it is not something to be intimidated by. From childhood onwards we are conditioned as a society to bench mark ourselves against other people and in business our performance is left wide open to public critique.

As a result we shy away from the prospect of our performance being judged. It comes back to the age old question *"What will people think of me?"* 'They are more qualified than me.' 'They are more skilled than me.' They are more popular than me.' etc. We question our performance and often our worth. What we fail to realise is that people in the business world are *people*! Business people are not some separate part of the human species; they are just normal people engaging in specific tasks. They too want to be liked and appreciated. They came into this world just as vulnerable as you did and believe it or not their personal concerns are similar to yours. Trust me I meet business people all the time. We all have the same human needs and we all have imbalanced lives, no matter what our roles are, no matter what qualifications we have, and no matter how financially wealthy we are. So you can be happy in the knowledge that you are as worthy and as capable as any other individual on this planet.

It's all about Who you Know!

You have probably heard the phrase "It's all about who you know in business that predicts business success." Perhaps you have even used that phrase at some point yourself. Let me tell you that it is not all about who you know in business that predicts successful relationships or good results. Having good connections is always good and indeed important but to become really successful in business you must understand and live from the following statement:

Business is not built just on who you know; it is built on who knows you and how good you are at building relationships.

Imagine for a moment that I work with a big company on a contract basis. I know who the CEO is and I see them regularly at business events. Based on the "It's all about who you know in business that predicts business success" principle, how does my knowing who the CEO is influence my business success? It doesn't! It is only when I become known to them that an opportunity for creating a business relationship opens up. You must become *visible and desirable* to know.

This is a three part process. For the purpose of making it easy for you to remember, we will refer to the process here as **PEM**. **P**resent, **E**stablish, **M**aintain.

Present

They say that to judge someone by appearance is a terrible thing "Never judge a book by its cover". That is a nice ideal but so far from reality. Albeit a bit shallow, we judge people all the time. In fact, research shows that we make a judgment on people we meet for the first time within just three seconds!

Yes, three seconds! If you don't believe me, imagine this scenario: It is late at night and you go alone to a cash dispenser to withdraw money. The area is quiet. Waiting behind you is a dirty scruffy man in his early twenties. He fidgets and shuffles from side to side. How do you think an average person might feel in this situation? Wouldn't it be understandable to feel nervous or even scared, to assume that the money is at risk of being taken? Most people would feel nervous in such a situation, yet nothing is known about the man whatsoever. We make a judgment based on his initial presentation.

If you want to come across well, you better make it so the judgment made about you within that three second judgement period is a good one! People will judge you even if you think they shouldn't. How do you present yourself? What message do you convey? Does your message reflect your business goal?

How to Present:

1. *Dress like you care.* It gives the impression of respect.
2. *Remember that you are your business.* The impression that you make on people is the impression they will have of your business.
3. *Shake Hands with Confidence***.** Always offer your hand *first* when being introduced to someone. It conveys confidence. Make the handshake firm

and assured, not limp. There is nothing worse than a limp handshake. Think of shaking someone's hand as a way of letting a person know you are present and worthy of knowing.

Establish

After your initial presentation your aim should be to establish a connection.

How to establish a connection:

1. *Be fully present.* There is nothing worse than having a conversation with someone who is only "half there". Become aware of the people you interact with. Listen, show interest in what they are saying and respond.
2. *Create an experience.* Allow people to feel important and to feel positive around you. The easiest way to do this is to show interest and ask open ended questions. For example, you might ask "What do you enjoy most about what you do?" Let them talk about something they feel good about. People love talking about themselves and about good experiences – they will tag the positive feeling to you.
3. *Stand out.* People aren't going to remember everything about you so make it easy for them to remember the key elements about you and your business.

- Your name
- Your company name
- Your business/industry (in three words or less)
- Your product
- Your location

The key is to find ways to unobtrusively increase the occurrence of these things in your conversation. Does your business have an unusual name? What's the story behind it? Have you a memorable tag line that reflects what you do? Is there anything current happening in the location of your business that could make your location memorable? For example, Karl is the cinematographer at Sunset Studios in LA, the same studios where a specific movie of interest was filmed. Look for an angle of interest.

4. *Create Value.* Some years ago during a conversation with business man, Pat Slattery, I learned the power of the question *"How can I help you?"* They are possibly the five most powerful words in business. It surprises people when someone actually wants to help them as most people only want to help themselves. So, the way it works is this: Listen to what they say during your conversation and then simply ask *How can I help you?* Obviously, only offer what you are prepared to do and can do.
5. *Follow Up!* When you meet someone that you would like to build a business relationship with

never assume that they will follow up with you after your initial conversation. Life takes over and people get busy. Don't take it personal if they don't contact you. Instead take a proactive approach and make sure you contact them. It is your responsibility to establish the connection. You do this in the following way:

- Make sure to get their business card before you part.
- Later that day (or the following day if it's late in the evening), send them a text or an email. For example, you might write something like "Hi Tom, It was lovely to meet you at the event this morning. Thank you for your time and I look forward to talking to you in the future. Best, Donna. " I have done this for years and it is a really effective way to create a good impression. It makes you stand out from the crowd. It makes you memorable. And importantly it creates an opportunity to connect again.

Maintain

There are five key elements to maintaining a good business relationship.

1. *Become Valuable.* People want to connect with people whom they feel can benefit from or who offer value to their lives and or business. Albeit a bit selfish, that's the way most people operate.

Think about ways you can create more value and become more valuable to know. Think about ways you can offer a better service or product. Raising your profile can also be beneficial. You might do this by contributing a regular feature to a magazine, speak at events, write a book etc.

2. *Under-Promise, Over-Deliver.* In business never guarantee perfection. Show that you strive for excellence but don't promise perfection. Instead, under-promise and over-deliver. When I work with people, they expect what I promise (it's made clear) but I always throw in a "bonus" that they do not expect to receive. It makes them feel special, like you went the extra mile for them. Bonuses could be anything from a gift item, a book, exclusive access to an event, or an introduction to an influential contact. Make it relevant and noticeable.
3. *Become Consistent.* Consistency builds trust and respect. Think about how you can ensure that you deliver every time.
4. *Show Gratitude.* As previously stated, gratitude is powerful and it will help you maintain a good relationship with people. It allows them to feel that you care, that you value and respect them – everyone wants to feel important. Your gratitude can be shown by a simple hand-written thank you card, by a personal phone call "just to say thank you for..." or a personal invitation to an event etc.

Keep it personal as it means more. It helps people feel important.

5. *Give Back*. Become a giver, not just a taker. Make everything you do a win-win and include other people in your goals. Having an attitude of gratitude makes this easy.

CHAPTER 9

Implement!

When you picked up this book you thought you wanted the confidence to succeed, but as you now know confidence and success are not things you can get or have; they are moment-to-moment feelings and results from doing certain things well and doing them often. You must create new habits to change how you feel and to improve your performance. As such, make your goal a must! It's time to decide, commit and take action on what you want and deserve. So, what is that something that you would love to feel confident doing but have prevented yourself doing up to now? What does success mean to you? Do you want to be good at interacting with people? Do you want to feel confident giving public speeches? Do you want to feel able to assert yourself? Do you want to start a company or a new job? Do you want to be wealthier? Do you want to be healthier? Do you want to try something new? Whatever it is, bring it into your mind now and make it a possibility.

Clarifying what you want

Research has shown time and again that people who write down what they want in detail are more likely to achieve their goals than people who don't. Not only that, it has been shown that people who write down goals achieve them quicker. This is one reason why I asked you to complete the written exercises in this book. Writing down your goals allows for neural pathways to be established and strengthened so your outcomes and new behaviours become habitual and automatic. You see, I don't want you to waste another moment playing small. You deserve to reach your potential. So, together we have already started the process of you becoming more confident and successful. Right now, your brain is already working on creating your new habits and behaviours so that your dreams become a reality!

Positive Statements

Make sure that when you're writing your goals you do so in the *positive* form only. For example, instead of writing 'I *don't want* to be afraid of public speaking any more...' write 'I want to be a very confident public speaker...' Your brain will work on your goal more effectively this way. It is clear direction and will give your brain laser-like focus. How will your goal's achievement look? What and who will be there? What will you hear? What good things will people say? How great will you feel? Write it down now.

My Goal

The Why

Put a reason behind your goal. Giving your brain a *Why* is the motivating factor for immediate strategy application. It will help you achieve a goal quicker and it will help you maintain the outcome. It's very difficult to establish or maintain anything if we put no purpose behind it. How much quicker and easier do people get in shape if they have a wedding or a vacation coming up? You see, we do things when we have a reason to do them, not just because they benefit us. Ask yourself *why* you want to achieve your goal. Why is it important to you? What will it mean for you and those around you when you feel more confident and when you are getting better results?

In addition to that, identify the benefits of achieving your goal. Create a positive emotional association around it. What good things will it do for you? What good things will it do for the people around you? This is very important and will help you maintain results long term. When your brain realises that achieving your goal is important and has benefits, it will want to achieve it!

My Why

____

____

____

____

The Benefits of Achieving my Goal

Stepping Stones

To make this goal attainment process as easy as possible for you we need to track and measure your progress as you hit your targets. Tracking and measuring will keep you focused and it will also help you feel accomplished as you reach your targets. We will make this easy for you by breaking down your goal into manageable steps. You may have your own targets but for the purposes of demonstrating how this exercise works, we will complete a 6 month template here. So, I want you to think of something you would like to feel confident doing in 6 months from now. Think of your successful outcome and in the box below write that 6 month goal, i.e. how you would like to feel and what would you like to be doing 6 months from now?

My 6 Month Goal

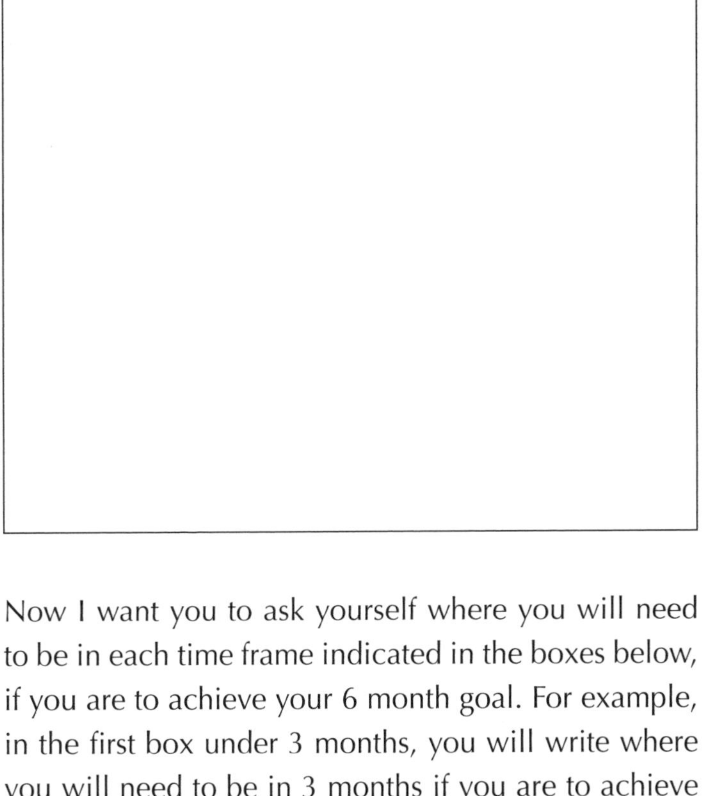

Now I want you to ask yourself where you will need to be in each time frame indicated in the boxes below, if you are to achieve your 6 month goal. For example, in the first box under 3 months, you will write where you will need to be in 3 months if you are to achieve your 6 month goal. In the next box under 1 month you will write where you will need to be in 1 month's time if you are to achieve your 6 month goal. In the next box you will write where you need to be in 1 week if you are to achieve your 6 month goal. You can refer back to the exercises you have already completed in the book if you need to further clarify what you want.

3 months	1 month	1 week

Once you have completed your weekly goal, I want you to get really specific. Doing ordinary small steps daily will make your goal very attainable. Remember, extraordinary things happen by doing lots of ordinary things!

Today Q. What Action do I need to take today to reach my 1 week goal?

When you have filled in your template put it somewhere where you can refer to it often. This will keep you focused on the bigger picture and the stepping stones you need to get there. The best way to do this is to invest in a page-a-day diary and stick your completed template in the inside cover. You will use this diary daily to fill in your action steps, ticking off each little goal as you achieve it each day. The daily small goals, the stepping stones, are very important. Keep your action steps simple and consistent. You will be confident to succeed!

Model Success

When I made the decision to become confident and successful I decided to find people who already had the result I wanted and see how they were doing it. I figured it might quicken things up for me. I thought of it in terms of following a good recipe. If I knew the ingredients and how to use them and then took action as instructed, I should come up with the result indicated in the recipe book, or at least something very similar. This was one of the most powerful things I ever chose to do, so much so that I still do it.

I read about people who had what I wanted, I watched and listened to their programmes, I signed up to their newsletters, I emailed them and I even wrote handwritten letters to some of them. I did whatever it took to learn their strategies. As I got more confident, I went to events they were speaking at, sometimes with the aim of getting a one-to-one meeting so I could pick their brains. I was a sponge for knowledge. And in appreciation for that knowledge, I took daily action.

You Can Do It!

I understand that implementing action steps toward a new goal can seem daunting. However, if at any time you feel your enthusiasm dipping, just acknowledge the feeling as normal (we all have off days) and let it go. Focus on the benefits of achieving your goal. Affirm *"I can and I will (fill in your goal). Now stay focused."* Write this affirmation on an affirmation card if you like and hang it somewhere you see often or indeed inside your diary.

Taking Action Now

It's time now for you to step up and be who you deserve to be. This is your opportunity to be, do and have whatever you want. This is your opportunity to get confident and stay confident. You have everything you need in this book to do it; all it's down to now is whether you will put what I've given you into action or not. It is only when you take action that things will change. You are well able to make this happen.

Create and Cultivate Momentum

The Recumbent Bike

Think of achieving your goal as cycling a recumbent bike (the bikes that are used in Spin classes). Initially when you get on, it can be tough to get the wheels spinning; you have to expend a little energy and work against some resistance, but once you push past those first few tough seconds and gather *momentum* it's easy, and soon your legs are spinning away using way less energy than it took to get started. Those confident people you see with lots of friends, those confident people you see at a podium or on TV, those confident people who can assert themselves easily – they are just regular people like you who made a decision to be better, took action, and practiced over and over until feeling confident became automatic.

Here are some ways that you can create momentum.

1. *Decide What You Want*

   Make sure you complete *every* exercise in this book. If you skimmed over any of the exercises, return to them now and complete them in full. It will give you clarity about what you want.

2. *Focus on What is Possible*

   Life is life so you can expect to meet obstacles along the way. However, don't go looking for them and don't create them! Keep your focus on what you *can* do and what *is* possible, not on what you can't do. Take that one next step, no matter how small, that will move you forward toward your successful outcome. Think of it as driving a car: when we drive a car we don't focus on the potholes in the road and we don't look backwards, instead we focus on our destination and we deal with whatever comes our way on the journey. You will get there!

3. *Picture Great Results*

   Remember, if you want something, visualise it. If you can't already see it in your mind's eye, how can you really and truly go after what you want? Give your brain crystal clear instruction. Make it real. A useful way to do this is to create a collage using visual cues such as pictures or pictures of words that trigger a positive emotional response. It will inspire you for action and keep you focused. Place it somewhere you'll see it every day, maybe on your fridge or phone screen saver. Look at the visual cues often and really absorb them. It's a matter of taking a few seconds out of your day (in the morning before you get out of bed, or before you go to sleep at night) to imagine yourself feeling confident and doing the things you want to do. Connect with it and evoke all your senses.

4. *Avoid Trying to do Everything at Once*
   To maintain momentum, it's important to break your main goal into small, manageable steps as we have just done. Take action, one step at a time, every single day. You will avoid the overwhelm of the main goal by deconstructing it into digestible parts. For example, if you are afraid of public speaking you might first try a little presentation to yourself aloud, then give the presentation to someone you trust, then to a group of four or five people and so on, until eventually you feel confident to speak in front of a large group. When I was afraid to be around people I had to take things very slow. My family was a huge support in helping me, in that they took me for drives and short walks so I could get used to being around people again, before I actually mingled with them etc.

5. *Understand What it Takes to Keep You Motivated*
   Reward yourself every time you achieve a goal, no matter how small. Acknowledge your successes. It doesn't have to be anything huge, just acknowledge how well you did. As you acknowledge your successes, your sense of confidence will soar.
6. *Surround Yourself with as Many Positive People as You Can*
   Surround yourself with people who think productively, people who are supportive, positive and confident at the things you want to be confident in. Being around supportive people is inspiring and helps you raise the bar for yourself. Their goals don't have to be the same as yours but being around them will give you a regular reminder that you can achieve your goal and it will help you to focus on your achievements.
7. *Live Without Excuses*
   Bottom line: there are *always* excuses but don't live them. There will always be too little time, too many commitments, and too many people pulling you in too many directions. Prioritise your wellbeing and the rest will happen so much more easily.
8. *Practice, Practice, Practice!*
   The more you practice doing the things you want to be able to do the easier it will be for you to do

them. Just keep focused and continue *doing* it! If you experience a hiccup, so what, get back up and practice more. Even if you have to do something a hundred times, keep doing. You will eventually get the result you want.

9. *Review your Overall Progress Regularly and Reorient Toward your Goal*
   If you get sidetracked stop, review what you are doing, adjust the plan if needed (may be you need help, a new skill etc.) and reorient to your successful outcome.
10. *Embrace it and Think Long Term*
   Once you really get some momentum going, don't be afraid of it. Instead, feel good about it and embrace it. Once you've started and gained a little momentum, you'll find that it will get easier each time to take the actions you need to take. You will feel more and more confident. You will find that all it will take is a little push every now and then to keep the momentum going. For example, I no longer need to practice public speaking in front of one person or a small group but to make sure I stay on form I ask for regular feedback from my positive peers and refine my presentations if needed. When it comes to goal execution, the key is to just keep on embracing, doing and refining.

Take Action TODAY!

You were born to be confident and successful! Start the ball in motion *now*. Don't wait. The seconds of your life are ticking away with each breath you take. What one small action can you take now that will help you to become more confident? Do it! You can be, do and have what you want. Believe in YOU!

www.donnakennedy.com